Nifty Thrifty Dentists

Praise for *Nifty Thrifty Dentists*

Dr. Glenn Vo has taken the dental world and reimagined it to create a new world that many influencers follow! You won't meet a more abundant human who looks out for all parties involved. Sign up now for anything he offers. I did over half a decade ago and I have not looked back.

—**ELIJAH "DJ SMILES" DESMOND**, CEO, HYPE Events

In *Nifty Thrifty Dentists*, Dr. Glenn Vo offers an invaluable road map for dentists seeking to elevate their practice through strategic, thoughtful leadership and operations. Throughout the book, Dr. Vo distills complex concepts into actionable advice that is both accessible and profound, and I have no doubt you will find tremendous value from it no matter how long you've practiced. In fact, despite my long-standing friendship with Glenn, diving into this book was an eye-opening experience and I learned quite a bit that will help me in my businesses.

—**DR. CHRIS HOFFPAUIR**, CEO,
Doc Hoff Investments LLC

Dr. Glenn Vo's contributions to the dental industry are unique and unmatched. His Nifty Thrifty Dentists community has given dentists a voice and pathway for success. I've been astounded by his innovative approach and consistent success. But the best measure of Glenn is who he is as a person. He's genuine, fun, and the type of person who blesses the lives of the people who know him.

—**DR. ERIC J. ROMAN**, dental key opinion
leader, founder, 1Life System

Dr. Glenn Vo isn't your typical dental entrepreneur; he's a compassionate trailblazer with a heart of gold. *Nifty Thrifty Dentists* is a testament to his passion for transforming lives and his unwavering commitment to innovation. Glenn is a true friend and mentor, always ready to uplift and inspire those around him. Through his genuine kindness and infectious enthusiasm, he's not just shaping smiles; he's empowering others to shine their brightest.

—**DR. ANISSA HOLMES**, founder of Delivering WOW Dental Education, cofounder of DentalFlix

Dr. Glenn Vo 's wisdom and business acumen have been pivotal in shaping not just my dental practice but also my broader entrepreneurial endeavors. He exemplifies the rare ability to blend clinical expertise with astute business strategy, an approach that has been invaluable to my own professional journey.

—**DR. BOB "DEE" DOKHANCHI**, Founder of Dentistry In General

Dr. Glenn Vo is someone I admire as a dentist, dad, and connector of "dentisting" humans. From his massive social media group, designed to help dentists build the business skills we do not learn in school to creative podcasting events, Dr. Glenn Vo offers dentists the opportunity to succeed and create a positive impact on the profession. I highly recommend *Nifty Thrifty Dentists*.

—**DR. PAUL GOODMAN**, founder, Dental Nachos

In his insightful and engaging book, *Nifty Thrifty Dentists*, Dr. Glenn Vo provides practical and effective answers, using his own journey as a successful practitioner and entrepreneur, yet saving more time, energy and preserving your mental health.

—DR. KATHRYN ALDERMAN

Glenn has a deep understanding of patient and provider needs, which gives him a competitive edge in identifying key technology innovations that can optimize a dental practice's workflow.

—DR. JEREMY KRELL, managing partner, Revere Partners

I'm constantly impressed with how Glenn reinvests himself to serve more dentists. He stays on top of business trends, but, more importantly, he executes them well. His writing is no exception and *Nifty Thrifty Dentists* is no exception. If you're looking to grow your business, this is your guide.

—AUSTIN HAIR, managing partner, Leaders Real Estate

Dr. Glenn Vo is not only an exceptional dentist but also a remarkable entrepreneur and human being. His genuine care and commitment to nurturing connections make him a standout in the dental field. And his multifaceted expertise and compassionate approach are truly inspirational.

—JONATHAN RAT, CEO, Archy

Dr. Glenn Vo is a down-to-earth, authentic, and respectable resource to everyone in the dental community. He's someone I respect very much, and I'm very grateful for all the help he provided to me. If you're looking to improve your practice and your life, *Nifty Thrifty Dentists* is the book to get you there.

—**DR. PAUL ETCHISON**, *Dental Practice Heroes Podcast*

I commend how much Dr. Glenn Vo has mastered building a brand outside of clinical dentistry to support those who are still working in clinical care. When I wrote my first consumer dentistry book in 2009, I didn't have an industry insider in publishing and multimedia to help me, but now Glenn has become that resource. His expertise and commitment to excellence are elevating the dental game!

—**DR. CATRISE AUSTIN**, celebrity dentist and celebrity branding coach, Celebrity Branding, LLC

Dr. Glenn Vo's thirst for knowledge, entrepreneurial savvy, dedication and generosity to others, and love of family and friends come shining through in everything he says, writes, and does. Get *Nifty Thrifty Dentists*, read it, and keep it in your library. It is a treasure trove of wisdom!

—**DR. ALAN STERN**, speaker, author, retired dentist, dental practice coach, Better, Richer, Stronger, LLC

From the first phone call I had with Dr Glenn Vo, I learned that not only was he the founder of Nifty Thrifty Dentist Group but he's a dental entrepreneur genius! After reading his book, *Industry Influencer,* I was able to take Glenn's words and apply them to further myself as a thought leader in the Dental Office Manager Industry. Dr. Vo is a true genuine friend whose integrity and kindness I deeply admire and cherish. I highly recommend *Nifty Thrifty Dentists.*

—**KYLE L. SUMMERFORD**, founder, Dental Office Managers Community

Dr. Glenn Vo has created a wonderful dental community full of abundance-minded professionals. His knowledge of what it takes to run a successful and profitable practice has helped thousands of dentists improve their bottom line. *Nifty Thrifty Dentists* is a must-read for anyone interested in lowering their overhead and increasing their EBITDA.

—**DR. ANDREW VALLO**, multi-practice owner and co-host of *Dental Unfiltered Podcast*

If you're sick of working way too hard for way too little money, Nifty Thrifty Dentists by Dr. Glenn Vo is for you. In this book, Dr. Vo will help you elevate your leadership, improve operations, and build a motivated, high-performing team.

—**DR. JONNY WITHANACHCHI**, principal and founder, Walk of Wealth

NIFTY

Thrifty

Dentists

Growing Your Practice by Prioritizing What Really Matters

DR. GLENN VO

NEW YORK

LONDON • NASHVILLE • MELBOURNE • VANCOUVER

Nifty Thrifty Dentists

Growing Your Practice by Prioritizing What Really Matters

Published in New York, New York, by Morgan James Publishing. Morgan James is a trademark of Morgan James, LLC. www.MorganJamesPublishing.com

Scriptures taken from the Holy Bible, New International Version®, NIV®. Copyright © 1973, 1978, 1984, 2011 by Biblica, Inc.™ Used by permission of Zondervan. All rights reserved worldwide. www.zondervan.com The "NIV" and "New International Version" are trademarks registered in the United States Patent and Trademark Office by Biblica, Inc.™

Proudly distributed by Publishers Group West®

Morgan James BOGO™

A FREE ebook edition is available for you or a friend with the purchase of this print book.

CLEARLY SIGN YOUR NAME ABOVE

Instructions to claim your free ebook edition:
1. Visit MorganJamesBOGO.com
2. Sign your name CLEARLY in the space above
3. Complete the form and submit a photo of this entire page
4. You or your friend can download the ebook to your preferred device

ISBN 9781636984780 paperback
ISBN 9781636984797 ebook
LCCN: 000000000000

Cover and Interior Design by:
Chris Treccani
www.3dogcreative.net

Morgan James is a proud partner of Habitat for Humanity Peninsula and Greater Williamsburg. Partners in building since 2006.

Get involved today! Visit: www.morgan-james-publishing.com/giving-back

Table of Contents

Acknowledgments

First and foremost, I want to thank my Lord and Savior Jesus Christ, with whom all things are possible. "Be strong and courageous. Do not be afraid or terrified because of them, for the LORD your God goes with you; he will never leave you nor forsake you" (Deuteronomy 31:6 NIV).

I couldn't possibly thank everyone who has influenced me in a positive way in my life. If you have crossed paths with me in my dental career, please know that I am forever grateful for you.

I do want to specifically acknowledge a few groups of people who motivated or supported me in creating this book.

First, thank you to my wife, Susan, and my kids, Kylie and Jackson. You are the reason I do everything I do. This book would not exist without your continued support. So many dentists are going to build bigger, better, and more fulfilling careers because of that support.

Thank you to my mother for the unconditional love that only a mother can show her child. And thank you, Mom, for the many years of sacrifice you showed our family so that we can all pursue our dreams. Thank you to my father for giving me the opportunity to have a better life in America.

Thank you to my sisters, Brittany and An, for continuing to "have my back" and support me no matter what is going on in my life, whether it be good or bad.

Thank you to my two brothers, Dan and Long, for pushing me and giving me the motivation to excel.

Thank you to everyone who has supported me in the past, whether through mentorship, friendship, or sponsorship. I'll continue to work hard to make you proud.

Thank you to Mango Voice, Crazy Dental Prices, Duane Tinker, Jeff Guidie, Wade Myers, Sean Ryan, and Harsh Patel for your help in making this book a reality.

Thank you to those who have not been very supportive, as well. It's not easy stepping up to create content and resources that help others. Those who do inevitably find people who doubt them, hate them, or even wish them to fail. I view those people as a sign of progress, so thank you to any of my detractors out there for giving me extra motivation to keep going.

Finally, thank you to David Hancock and the entire Morgan James Publishing team. You continue to help me make my dreams a reality, and I look forward to many more collaborations in the future.

Foreword by Kevin Tallman,
CEO of Mango Voice

Building a business is demanding. It will test you in ways that you don't understand. The emotional roller coaster of daily demands and decisions can test even the most seasoned entrepreneur. For the last fifteen years, I have been committed to building businesses. Through this journey, I've come to realize that finding the right partners and mentors can be a lifeline in the turbulent sea of leadership.

In my years of experience, I've learned that getting the fundamental aspects of leadership and business management right is key to determining the long-term value you create. I frequently see leaders and business managers missing the mark on critical elements of running a business such as culture, accountability, building strategic relationships, and a complete lack of understanding of the numbers that drive your business. In many ways, they are in the middle of a game blindfolded. This often leads to burnout, dysfunction, and value destruction. Learning these principles and applying them become paramount for success. At

Mango, we are fortunate to have an incredible team and partners who have bought into our long-term vision.

I first heard the name Glenn Vo in the spring of 2017. My business partner and I had recently invested in a company called Mango Voice. We had no prior experience in the dental industry, and the nuance of the dental market was new to us. I knew that we needed to find strategic partners who would guide us through the maze. Very early on, it became clear to me that Glenn Vo would play a pivotal role in Mango's success.

When Glenn reached out and talked to me about this book, I was excited that he was thinking about principles that I often see business owners and leaders struggling with. I am humbled and grateful that I have the privilege of writing this foreword. I consider Glenn a friend above all else. He has been in the trenches with me when times were looking bleak. He never gave up on us. In 2019 we encountered significant operational challenges that resulted in our system going offline. This was a challenging time for me and the entire Mango team. Glenn stood by our side, remained fully engaged, and played a pivotal role in helping us communicate in nearly real time to customers. It is said that you find out who your real friends are when things are at their worst. In that moment, I knew Glenn lived the principles he espoused and that we can count on him when the chips are down.

Through Glenn's visionary leadership and unwavering dedication to the dental profession, he has played an important part in transforming partnerships, social media, and other aspects of the market. Glenn's vision to build Nifty Thrifty Dentists has been invaluable for companies like ours to be able to tell our story and drive value to dental offices. It truly is a testament to his entrepreneurial vision and his commitment to helping others succeed.

In this book, Glenn shares his wealth of knowledge and experiences as an operator and leader. He delves into the key aspects of business leadership. He breaks down the steps of building effective leadership, running high-functioning teams, and the indispensable art of knowing your numbers. These concepts are not just theoretical concepts; they are the bedrock of Glenn's success and have helped him and countless others achieve extraordinary gains.

In today's business landscape, true leadership is rare—individuals and organizations who not only lead but inspire and drive progress. Even more rare is finding partners who view business and relationships in the same strategic light. To me, Glenn embodies these qualities. His unwavering commitment to his vision and his unselfish willingness to support those around him are what set him apart.

As you embark on the journey through the pages of this book, I encourage you to study and absorb Glenn's wisdom and apply the principles to your own endeavors. Whether you are an aspiring entrepreneur, a seasoned business leader, or anyone looking to enhance their business and leadership skills, Glenn's insights will undoubtedly prove invaluable.

I am immensely proud to call Glenn Vo my friend. I am confident that his book will leave a lasting impact on all who read it. Prepare to be inspired, enlightened, and motivated to reach for new heights in your own journey.

Here's to Glenn Vo, a true leader and an exceptional friend.

KEVIN TALLMAN
CEO, Mango Voice

Introduction

The Nifty Thrifty Dentist and Prioritizing What Really Matters in Your Business and in Your Life

> **Nif·ty /** ˈniftē/ adjective: particularly good, skillful, or effective.[1]
>
> **Thrift·y /** ˈThriftē/ adjective: using money and other resources carefully and not wastefully.[2]

I grew up in a very traditional Vietnamese family, with five kids in addition to my mom and dad. Although I grew up in the US, my family ate a lot of Vietnamese food. My dad loved Vietnamese food the most. I enjoyed it, but I wanted to eat cheeseburgers like all of my friends. Every once in a while, my mom would take me and my

---

1 Oxford Languages, s.v. "nifty (adj.)," accessed March 3, 2024, https://www.google.com/search?q=nifty+meaning&oq=nifty+def.

2 Oxford Languages, s.v. "thrifty (adj.)," accessed March 3, 2024, https://www.google.com/search?q=thrifty+definition&oq=thrifty+def.

four siblings to McDonald's, but for the most part, dinner was Vietnamese food. I didn't know at the time, but there was more than one reason we didn't eat cheeseburgers very often.

On the rare instances we got to eat cheeseburgers, however, I noticed something strange, even as a young child. Specifically, although we had a McDonald's right next to our house, my mom would take me and my four siblings to another McDonald's location across town to get cheeseburgers.

I didn't think too much about it other than it was strange that we would drive across town with a McDonald's right next to our house. Then, as I got older, I noticed that my mom frequently spoke with the manager when we went there, so I figured she must have been friends with him and wanted to visit her friend.

I didn't learn the real reason we went to that McDonald's until I was an adult. After shopping at a grocery store, I noticed a bunch of coupons on the back of the receipt, including offers for fast-food restaurants. At that moment, I flashed back to my childhood and remembered my mother used to carry a bunch of receipts with her.

Curious, I decided to ask my mother about those coupons. "Do you remember getting coupons on the back of grocery receipts?" I asked.

That's when she told me that all those receipts I remembered had "buy one, get one free Big Mac" coupons on the back of them.

It turns out that sometimes my parents would have a hard time making ends meet. That included having a tough time getting food on the table. My dad was an electrician and my mom worked as a gas station attendant, but with five kids to take care of, they would sometimes run out of money before the end of the month.

Because of that, my mom kept a stack of buy one, get one free Big Mac coupons at all times. Whenever we were having trouble making ends meet, my mom would take us across town to that McDonald's because the manager had told her he would let her use as many coupons as she wanted. Normally there's a limit of one coupon per customer. But he saw her come in with five kids and told her she could use three coupons when ordering six Big Macs. At the time, the cost of three Big Macs was a lot less than groceries to feed a family of seven for the night, and those coupons helped a lot. My siblings and I loved going to McDonald's and thought of it as a treat. But to my parents, those trips, and the manager's generosity, were more than a treat. They were a necessity to help us make it until my dad got his next paycheck and we could go back to eating our normal groceries or his cherished Vietnamese food.

What does this have to do with running a "Nifty Thrifty" dental practice? Growing up, being nifty and thrifty was a way of life for my family. It was something many families did back then too. As a child, I neither learned nor appreciated just how much my mom and dad sacrificed for us kids to be successful. But on reflection, I'm amazed by how well they stretched their limited resources in a way that gave their five children a better life without us even realizing it. My siblings and I were never wasteful or anything like that. But we never felt like money was a significant challenge for my parents.

That's really what building a Nifty Thrifty dental practice is all about: being good, skillful, and effective with your resources, using them carefully and not wastefully. And when you do it right, your team members, patients, vendors, and family will feel just like my siblings and I did growing up: happy, fulfilled, and well taken care of.

Today, even as someone who runs a successful dental practice and community for dentists, I keep the spirit of being nifty and thrifty close to my heart because I know how impactful it can be. By being wise with money and other resources and skillful in how we serve patients, I am able to add even more value to my patients and team members because I'm not wasting time and money. And I can free up time and profits to make sure I take care of my family too.

Being nifty and thrifty is not just a practice principle either. I try to reflect these principles in everything I do and never forget my upbringing. For example, when I see people eating fast food, I don't judge them. They might be struggling to make ends meet. You might think that someone who is a dentist and medical professional like me would accuse them of being unhealthy, but I have a different perspective. I grew up eating Big Macs from time to time because that's all we could afford. If there had been a coupon for Jack in the Box or Taco Bell, I'm sure my mom would have cut that out and fed us at one of those places. She and my dad did what they had to do to put food on the table for their children.

What It Means to Be a Nifty Thrifty Dentist

Because of my family's experience, I often think back to the immigrant mindset when it comes to being nifty and thrifty. I think of my parents' place of struggle, and it reminds me to be intentional with my own resources. I maintain this mindset even though I'm in a place in which I am fortunate to not have to worry about putting food on the table. My wife and I have built a successful dental practice and invested intentionally in several business ventures.

But just because you aren't in a place of struggle doesn't mean it's not smart to be careful with your resources. Just because you don't have to drive across town to find a manager who allows you to use multiple coupons at a time doesn't mean it's wise to overspend unnecessarily. Just because your practice is consistently profitable doesn't mean it is not worth adopting the mindset of being nifty and thrifty in what you do.

But what does it mean to be a "Nifty Thrifty" dentist?

When I mention my Nifty Thrifty Dentists community to people, their first thought is often that the community is all about spending or being "cheap." While it's true that a small percentage of what I do for our community involves helping practices save money, being a Nifty Thrifty dentist is about much more than spending. And it is certainly not about being cheap.

Being a Nifty Thrifty dentist involves using the definitions of both of the words, nifty and thrifty—in that order—as a filter through which you make decisions in your practice. If you do, you'll find that nowhere in the definitions does it say to be "cheap."

So what does that filter look like?

It starts with being nifty, which means particularly good, skillful, or effective. In the context of a dental practice, that means making sure whatever you do starts with quality as a goal. Nifty Thrifty dentists are good owners, effective leaders, and skillful clinicians. They build teams that are good, effective, and skillful in what they do. And they implement effective systems, invest wisely in quality materials, and build effective relationships with suppliers and other vendors.

In addition to the pursuit of quality, Nifty Thrifty dentists are thrifty, using money and other resources carefully and not wastefully. Notice that nowhere in that definition will you find the word "cheap." Being thrifty is not about saving money. In fact, sometimes it means spending *more* money than others, especially with quality being the goal. But we make decisions about how we spend our important resources of time and money intentionally with the goal of not wasting either.

By the end of this book, my goal is to give you everything you need to be the niftiest, thriftiest dentist around, to build a practice that fills not just your bank account but also your sense of joy, purpose, and peace of mind. What's more, I want to make sure you have everything you need to continue to build upon what I share in this book so you can continue to build toward an even more profitable and fulfilling practice completely independent from me or any other practice mentor.

I want to teach you how to fish, not just give you a few fish to boost your profits this quarter and get you excited about the future while leaving you vulnerable over the long term.

I want you to *want* to work with me, stay active in the Nifty Thrifty Dentists Facebook community, or follow my podcast, website, or other channels. I don't want you to *need* to.

That's my goal for you.

You're Working Too Hard

Like you, I came to this profession with a unique background. Perhaps you are the child of a dentist (or two). Or maybe you're the first one in your family to go to college or receive a professional degree. Or maybe you're the child of immigrants who struggled to make ends meet like I am. Whatever your background, there's nobody who shares your exact path to where you are today. However, after helping thousands of practices, dentists, and other dental professionals over the years, there's one fact I've observed in every single practice that I can confidently say I know about you even if we've never met: you're working too hard.

But what does it even mean to work too hard? Too many hours? Not enough money for the hours you're working? Too stressed throughout the day? Too rushed with patients to the extent that it's only a matter of time before you mess something up? Performing too many tasks that someone in your position should not be performing? Unable to get your practice off your mind when you're home? Something else? A combination of these? All of them?!

The truth is, I've never met someone in dentistry who isn't experiencing more than one of these challenges, or others. Dentists are working way too hard.

That was me, for a long time, too, especially when I first opened my practice, although I'm thankful that my upbringing instilled in me natural instincts to work smarter, not harder—creative with both my time and my money. I was fortunate to learn from my parents' struggles, so I came into the profession with experience and a mindset that it takes many dentists years of struggle to develop. I came in questioning the way business was done in dentistry, not just accepting the old adage that dentistry is different from any other business. Together, my experience and mindset made me develop what I'd later describe as a "Nifty Thrifty" mindset from the very beginning in my practice.

It didn't take long for me to realize this Nifty Thrifty mindset was more than just watching numbers and looking for deals. It gave me a filter through which I made sure I knew exactly how to find and treat patients, how to create a high-quality office environment and experience, how to build a happy, productive team, and how to achieve more security in terms of time and money for me and my family. For these reasons, and more, I'm forever grateful for what I learned from my parents' struggle.

As fate would have it, my Nifty Thrifty mindset may have been my greatest asset when I opened up my dental practice as a start-up in 2009 at the height of the biggest housing and financial crashes since the Great Depression.

For those who experienced the 2009 crash, I don't have to describe it to you. The very mention of 2009 probably brings a sinking feeling to your gut. You know how scary that time was for a lot of people and how devastating it was to a lot of businesses.

Fortunately, my experience was quite different from many dental practices and other businesses. As many people around me were going into bankruptcy and foreclosure, I opened a successful business, and being nifty and thrifty is what got me through that difficult time. It helped me grow a practice that gave me time and financial freedom to do so much more than many dentists think possible. It was so helpful and impactful for me that I started teaching others the principles and helping them implement them into their practices. Little did I know that, years later, that freedom to build what would become the Nifty Thrifty Dentists community would result in so much good for so many people in the industry, most notably in helping thousands of practices get through the COVID-19 pandemic while other offices struggled or shuttered.

As a reminder, being a Nifty Thrifty dentist is not about being cheap. It's not about being low quality. It's not about beating people up for discounts, cutting corners, or nickel-and-diming every vendor who walks into your office. It's about being skillful, intentional, and high quality, managing time and money with the mindset of an investor, investing time and money where it can have the highest impact on your vision, and not dedicating resources in areas that don't matter much.

A Nifty Thrifty dentist is good, skillful, and effective. They serve their patients well. And their team is happy to be a part of what they're doing. They keep up with the times, investing in technology and other areas that help them achieve practice goals, become more efficient, or provide a better, more reliable patient experience. They use their resources carefully and not wastefully, including money, mental bandwidth, and time. This is important because, no matter how much money you have in your bank account, you have limited mental bandwidth and time that you can leverage toward your growth and success.

And that's where I find way too many dentists are working much harder than they need to: with their time and mental bandwidth. In my experience, any dentist reading this book can make more money, have more time off, and free up more mental bandwidth, all while spending *less* money overall with a few tweaks to how they approach their practice.

That's what I want for you too: to use these principles to build a practice—and *life*—that you love.

The ISS Mentality

In their best-selling book, *The Bezos Letters: 14 Principles to Grow Your Business like Amazon*, authors Steve and Karen Anderson discuss how Amazon's "Day One" mentality to everything it does has allowed Amazon to grow intentionally and maintain several advantages over companies that become more wasteful or careless as they achieve greater financial heights.

Among other things, Amazon's Day One mentality calls for the company and all its team members to maintain the same mindset they used when they first started the company, when they couldn't just write a check to cover virtually any mistake but needed to be careful and deliberate with how they used their resources, treated customers, and so forth.

What I will refer to as the ISS Mentality encourages you to take a similar approach to your practice too. The I in ISS stands for Immigrant. The first S stands for Start-Up. The second S stands for Student. I use all three references because I know every dentist reading this book has experience with at least one of these. We've all been students, of course. But for those of us who have experienced what it's like to be an immigrant or be raised by immigrants, or those of us who have built a start-up practice, that experience might have had an even more profound impact on what we value and how we managed our time and money before. Those experiences, or your experience as a student, may have caused you to be more mindful, careful, or deliberate with your resources. That mentality can help you achieve great things if you apply it to your dental practice using what I will teach you in this book.

Everyone can adopt a mentality like this. Unfortunately, I've noticed that many dentists begin to dismiss or forget about this mentality once they start to become successful. It's understandable. They work so hard and just want to enjoy the fruits of their labor for a while. They start to have more than enough of what they need. They don't really have to worry about how much they're wasting and how much money is going out the door. Unbeknownst to them, however, they quickly find themselves in a place of comfort and complacency. And that very often develops into a slow-moving train to discomfort, stress, and frustration.

Is that something you want in your dental practice? Are you struggling to get by as a practice, or even struggling to connect with your family and personal life after long workweeks? What I'm going to share in the following pages can help you not only regain some of your personal and family time but also get better results in your practice.

How to Get the Most from This Book

This is not like the books that give you ten steps or some one-size-fits-all system and then tell you to force that system into your business. There's nothing wrong with those books, but I don't see those rigid systems as a recipe for success, especially with how many different types of practices there are or different goals you may have. Instead, I'll walk you through fifteen universal principles that can be adapted to help any practice achieve its goals. Then, I'll show you how to customize them for your specific goals and your specific practice so you can create what works best for you.

In fact, as you read this, you might even notice that the concepts aren't unique to dentistry itself. They work in any industry. Still, the important part is to apply them, see what works in your practice, and run with what works best. Of course, if you have questions along the way, join my Nifty Thrifty Dentists Facebook community and ask. I'm in there every day, along with tens of thousands of other dentists who are living the Nifty Thrifty principles.

For these reasons, when you're reading this book, I want you to focus mostly on the concepts, not the specific examples of how I'm using these processes in my practice or how other dentists have adapted them for theirs. You can't just take everything I'm doing, apply it to your practice, and assume you'll get the same exact results. Instead, adapt them to your unique situation, and I'm confident you can achieve even better results in your practice.

In fact, I would go so far as to say that that's why most books and processes fail to help people achieve their desired results. People try to read and copy cookie-cutter solutions. Authors try to "give readers a fish" instead of "teaching them to fish." And that leaves readers without the ability to think on their own. If something changes, they have to run back to the book or hire the author to tell them what to do next.

I don't want that for you. I want you to see hiring any coach as a "shortcut," not a necessity. If you want someone like me to help customize and implement principles in your practice, I want it to be because you want results faster, not because you aren't able to do it yourself.

Throughout this book, I will "give you" many fish. I'll share systems or specific strategies I and others have used. You can certainly customize and run with those. But I'm also going to teach you the underlying principles and concepts of each so you learn how to develop your own systems and strategies as well.

By the end of this book, I'm confident you won't need me in order to succeed. I'd love for you to *want* to become a part of my Nifty Thrifty Dentists community, participating in our discussions, benefiting from the deals I negotiate on your behalf with suppliers, vendors, and others, and even helping to lead the next generation of Nifty Thrifty dentists. But I want you to *want* to be a part of the community. I don't want you to *need* it in order to succeed.

The Big Picture

Over the rest of the book, I'm going to divide the principles into three important categories.

First, I'm going to help you develop into a Nifty Thrifty dentist and business owner. The principles in this first section will help you work on yourself. This is where you learn how to adopt an owner mindset—how to improve your leadership, your skills, and your personal growth. Ultimately, you'll shift from being a dentist who works the operatory to a dentist who works the board-room (if only mentally).

Second, I'm going to help you develop a Nifty Thrifty team. The principles in the second section will help you build your team into one of the most productive, fulfilled, and motivated teams around. We will look at your team's mindset, how your recruiting works, how your compensation model works, your training and retention strategies, and more.

In the third part of the book, we dive deep into Nifty Thrifty operations, helping you understand your numbers, analyze your spending, negotiate win-wins, and set up your business for growth—without you having to burn the candle at both ends.

The beauty of this process is you don't need to master all of the principles to be successful. Being intentional and consistent with them, along with making a commitment to be a continuous learner, is all you need to do to start benefiting as a Nifty Thrifty dentist. The more you do it, the more you benefit. But you don't have to wait to start benefiting. In fact, many practice owners can benefit in multiple ways immediately upon implementing one or two principles.

My hope for you is that this book helps you become better at what you do, not just so you can make more money but also so you can be more available for your family, so that you can be more attuned to yourself, and so that you can grow as a person and get meaning and value out of life. You'll use your dental practice as a vehicle to your personal vision and purpose, rather than using your dental practice as the be all, end all.

If that's something you want, join me on the rest of this journey.

Part 1:

Yourself

Chapter 1:

Owner Mindset

Houston, Texas, not too far from where I live, is home to one of the largest Asian populations in the nation, including Vietnamese, my heritage.

Living close to such a large Vietnamese community has been incredibly rewarding for me in many ways. I have many of the best Vietnamese restaurants around right in my backyard. And, yes, despite my childhood excitement when my mom would drive us across town for McDonald's, I developed a strong preference for Vietnamese food, especially pho, just like my father.

Among my favorite Vietnamese dishes is pho. And my favorite place to eat pho happens to be a hole-in-the-wall in the sketchy part of town. There are newer restaurants in nicer areas where I can get the same dish. But I love this place because the food is really good and the people are incredibly nice. I also love that this place is a hole-in-the-wall and not in a ritzy area of town.

Yet nearly every time I'm invited to dinner by a colleague, the restaurant they choose is a fancy or stuffy restaurant in a ritzy area. Why do you think that is? Some people truly love fancy restaurants, of course. They enjoy dressing up, getting ready, experiencing high-end service, and drinking expensive wine. They like to see and be seen. They get true joy from that experience. There's nothing wrong with that either. If that's what you love, great.

But other people choose fancy restaurants because they think that's what I want (without asking). Or they think that's what you need to do when it comes to business. They dread getting ready and hate "faking it" through a fancy dinner. They can't wait to get home, kick off their too-tight shoes, and collapse in bed, exhausted from their fancy dress or three-piece suit plus the mental gymnastics of navigating a fancy restaurant experience.

If you were trying to build a relationship with people in business, which approach do you think would be better? Of course, the fancy restaurant is the "safer" route. Your business partners will likely not think twice about you taking them to the local steakhouse, even if they end up mentally exhausted from the experience. They expect to. But savvy businesspeople take the time to learn more about their colleagues and customize an experience that will stand out and be memorable for their dinner partner.

Over the years of talking about my favorite pho restaurant, many people have confided in me that their favorite places to eat are hole-in-the-wall restaurants, and not some ritzy fancy place.

That doesn't mean you should build a hole-in-the-wall mindset when it comes to your practice or move to the sketchy part of town. But what it does suggest is that the "standard" approach to building an experience for yourself, your team, and your patients might not be the right approach for what *you* want for your practice *and* your life.

In this chapter, I'm going to help you shift your mindset away from looking at your practice with the mindset of what other people say you have to do and toward what *you* actually want.

Do you want to build a luxury, spa-like practice? Great! That goal can guide you as you make decisions. Do you enjoy PPO practices or serving lower-income families? That's great too. Whatever you desire, shift away from the mindset of "this is how dentistry is done" to the mindset of "this is what I want for my practice." Then match your decisions to that vision, spending time, money, and mental energy wisely when and where it makes a difference for your vision.

For example, I know plenty of dentists who want to build a practice based on quality. They want high-quality service, supplies, and materials. They want patients to not worry about quality when they walk through the doors because the practice is committed to high-quality everything.

To that end, they invest a lot of money on top-quality supplies and equipment. There's nothing wrong with that, of course. But does that mean they need to buy top-of-the-line everything? Does *every* supply make a difference? What about cotton balls? What about gloves? What about other supplies that get thrown away and are essentially commodities? I've worked with practice owners who seemingly automatically just buy top-of-the-line everything because they want quality, not realizing they could do so much more to provide for patients, team members, and the dentists who work with them if they tweaked their mindset to one of an owner, "spending time, money, and mental energy where it makes a difference given your goals," rather than as the typical purchasing agent, "spending based on routines, habits, and how they've always done it."

No matter what your vision is, your patient typically doesn't care what quality gloves you wear. They don't even know. They also typically don't care how expensive your cotton balls were. They care that the experience they receive matches what they expected when they walked in the door. If you market your practice as a "spa-like" practice, they expect a spa-like experience. If you present it as a "quality and convenience" practice, they expect longer opening hours and quick, quality service. If you market your practice as an "innovative" one, they expect new experiences and technology.

Going back to my favorite pho restaurant, the best meetings I have are almost always the ones with the people who focus on what I really want, rather than checking some "this is what a business meeting looks like" box.

Way too many dentists end up taking the "check the box" approach to their practice instead of asking themselves, "What does somebody really care about when it comes to dentistry and my practice?" or "What do my patients expect from my practice based on how I promote my practice or the type of practice we run?"

Then start making business decisions that align with those answers—rather than your personal preferences or what you think dental practices "must do." For example, your patients probably don't really care about having fancy gloves or top-of-the-line cotton balls. But they likely do care about having a nice clean bathroom. And if you promote your practice as a "spa-like" one, they probably care about nice scents in the bathroom. Patients also often do care about the furniture in your waiting room. Is it clean? Comfortable? If you promote yourself as a high-end or modern practice, are they modern or stylish? These are the things to consider spending money on because ultimately they are what is going to attract and retain the patients you want. And that will drive the revenue for your business.

But it all starts with your mindset. Do you have the mindset of a clinician, obsessed with all the newest tools or fancy gloves? Or do you have the mindset of an owner, identifying where it makes sense to buy high-end and where high-end doesn't make a difference to your patients? In this chapter, I'll walk you through a simple approach to developing an owner mindset.

Back to Basics

When I first opened my practice, I made a terrible mistake . . . or at least that's what everybody told me at the time. What did I do? I opened up my office on the second floor of an older strip mall. Yes, I know the three rules in real estate: location, location, location. And I know convenience is so important to customers. But I very intentionally chose a second-floor location in an older building in an area that wasn't in high demand.

Why? If you remember, I opened my practice in 2009, at the height of the Great Recession. I had a realtor who was looking all around for locations for me to have my dental practice. And I ended up finding my location by myself. The reason I found it was because it was a building right off the highway. As you drove by, you could see the building, and because it was on the second floor, it was right there. And the exit closest to it took you to a relatively old shopping center.

I ended up pulling off the highway one day and talking to the landlord, just inquiring. He told me that they had never had a tenant up there because businesses don't enjoy being on the second floor. And he was right. In fact, there are a lot of reasons why a business might not set up on the second floor.

Patients want to be on the ground floor. They don't want to have to walk up and down stairs, or God forbid, take an elevator. A business doesn't want to be on the second floor because they might have to carry their business equipment up the stairs.

So I ended up going with this location, even though my realtor was trying to discourage me from it.

I was going off basic business principles. I found this building very easily just by driving on the highway. It was very easy to get to just by pulling off at the nearest exit. So it had high visibility and high ease of location. Awesome. Next, it had very favorable rent because no business wanted to be on the second floor. The landlord was very eager to get *anybody* up into that space because they were losing money on it.

And so there's the story. I started out my business by being nifty and thrifty.

It was an older shopping center, it was very cheap rent, and it was a building that could be seen from the highway by thousands and thousands of people every single day. So I set to work, making sure the inside of the office and the bathrooms looked nice. Then, I put a big sign on the outside of the building advertising the dental practice.

After that, something ridiculous happened: *people started coming in.*

So from the very first quarter of my business, I have been profitable.

People make the argument against being on the second floor or being in an older shopping center because they think that they're going to get business from foot traffic. But the truth is a lot of people will find your business driving on the highway, or they'll find your business online or in the yellow pages, and then they'll come in. By the time they book an appointment with you and get all the way to your practice, hardly anyone will care whether the business is on the second floor. But these are the kinds of thoughts that consume us when we try to get Fancy Schmancy instead of Nifty Thrifty.

In my time, I've noticed way too many dentists wanting to set up shop on the ground floor in the newest, fanciest part of town, in a fancy schmancy shopping center right next to upscale purse stores. And then they are curious why no one is walking in.

So again, go back to being nifty and thrifty. We're talking about being skillful. We're talking about saving money.

Tried and True

When I first tried to get patients, it was 2009. As you may remember, the economy wasn't doing so well. I had just made this investment into having a dental office in this new place. So, I went back to tried-and-true business principles to get people in the door.

A lot of times we either overcomplicate the sales and marketing side of our business or we push our energy into places that don't really give us a return. Instead, I leveraged what I had at that moment. I didn't have a ton of money for marketing because I didn't have any patients. What I did have was time and mental bandwidth. Those are the resources I had to use, so I took advantage of them.

I went to every healthcare practitioner store, every outpatient clinic I could find, and said, "Hey, I'm a new dentist in this area. I'd love to take care of your staff. Let's refer patients back and forth." I went to every business within driving distance and asked, "Do you have dental insurance?" And if they did, I would offer a discount plan for all their employees. This meant it would cost the business $0 to send people my way, and the employees at that business would also get a discount.

Whenever I made a relationship with a new business, I also would give the owner of that business a free examination and cleaning. This is the old way of marketing. I went out and I networked and I built relationships with the people. It was nifty and it was thrifty.

We often forget these basic principles. We want to do a bunch of Facebook or Google ads. We want to spend thousands of dollars filming a really cool video and putting it online. That's all well and good if you have money, but I guarantee you my practice grew much faster and much larger simply because I made relationships with people who counted—the healthcare practitioners and business owners in my area. It took no money at all, and I was profitable within the first quarter of opening my dental practice.

Think of it this way. You could spend $5,000 on Facebook ads in a video, or you could give $5,000 in discounts to people at the nearest local business, and your "ad spend" is going to be the same. But in one case, people are going to come in paying full price and initially be skeptical about your business. In the other case, people are going to be warmed up to you because you're giving them a discount, you're local, and you have a good relationship with their boss because of that free cleaning and examination.

Three Resources Everyone Has

So again, leverage the resource you have the most of. You have money, you have mental bandwidth, and you have time. If you have a lot of money and not a lot of time, maybe you do need to pay for standard advertising. But if you don't have a lot of money, but you have a lot of time because you're a new dentist, like I was, consider going old school.

I had a couple of months before I had my grand opening. This meant that I had an abundance of time, I had no money coming in the door, and all my bandwidth was focused on getting as many patients as I could within the next eight weeks. So I spent the time going out, talking to people, inviting people to come over, giving good experiences, and building relationships.

In fact, there was a very popular burger place right next to my business. So I popped over there, gave the owner the opportunity to come in, gave him a free cleaning, and he saw how it was. I gave him a discount on other services, and he's been a patient ever since. Where's the first place you think he recommends his employees to go when they need a dentist? He ended up becoming an ambassador for my business, and that's the difference between a regular dentist and a Nifty Thrifty dentist. Are you merely getting patients in the door, or are you building ambassadors for your dental practice? People love to work with people they feel comfortable with. And when you give somebody a good experience, they're going to turn around and share you with others.

In the very first month of my dental practice being open, we broke even. In the second month, we made a profit. That was in 2009. Ever since then, even during the height of the COVID-19 pandemic, we've been profitable. We've done this by adopting the owner mindset, leveraging our resources well, and being nifty and thrifty with our operating expenses.

You have to think outside the box for your context. For example, unlike me, you might have a practice on Billionaire's Row. A good strategy for you might be to market to those billionaires. You could offer flexible hours that enable them to come by your dental practice after hours. Since they're spending their Monday to Friday just working their butts off, and you enable them to squeeze in a dental appointment between work and going home to see their kids, they'll warm up to you quickly, then tell all their billionaire friends.

The important part is realizing what the customer actually wants and what will work for your context. Then, putting in the legwork.

Shift Your Mindset

It's very easy for a dentist to think that they want the best of everything because their patients are going to want the best of everything. Instead, you have to be thrifty. You have to be smart with your money. Think of it this way: if you're going to buy some tickets to the Boston Celtics, you could go buy them full price over at Ticketmaster, but a Nifty Thrifty Celtics fan will instead find some poor sap out there who needs to get rid of their tickets and is willing to sell them for a lower price.

That's looking for a good deal with everything you do. That's holding on tightly to every dollar you have going out of your business. It's asking yourself earnestly, "Is there a more cost-effective way to do this?" It's looking for every result you want to get in your business, like new patients, and asking yourself, "Is there a way that I can get this for free?"

Could you start forming relationships with business owners or healthcare practitioners around you? Could you set up your business or even a sign for your business in a place that has mega high visibility?

There isn't a direct relationship between the money you spend and the results you get, after all. The owner mindset instead flips and thinks about maximizing the results they can get for the money they spend.

To give a couple of real-life examples, I started putting TVs in my ceiling early. I was one of the very first dentists to do that. This is because I was thinking patient first. Would *you* rather look at your dentist's nose hairs or your favorite TV channel?

I also didn't get the super big Mercedes-Benz version of a chair; instead I got what you might call the Toyota Camry of dental chairs. But what I did was I decked those chairs out. I put some of the finest upholstery on them, and I made them look amazing and be super comfortable. And my patients had no idea that it was a relatively cheap chair because they were getting the finest experience as it was.

Simply put, having an owner mindset is understanding who pays your bills (the patient) and doing your best to make them comfortable and happy. So as a Nifty Thrifty dentist, that's where I spent my money at first.

Don't Overextend

The final part of adopting the owner mindset is realizing that you can't overextend.

I started out with five operatories, and I decided I would never grow beyond my capability to fill my chairs. A Nifty Thrifty dentist doesn't overextend themselves financially, and they don't overextend themselves personally or professionally.

We have the temptation as dentists to want to keep up with the Joneses, people we see at continuing education events. Don't fall into this trap. Always live beneath your means. Part of the reason that my dental practice has been profitable since the very beginning is because we always got what we could afford, no more. We didn't stress ourselves out by living close to our means or above our means at any point. Just because we can do something doesn't mean we have to. We don't always have to be Superman in our dental practice.

I recommend never overextending yourself personally either. If you have an opportunity to recharge and reset, always take it. Don't be that dentist who spends nine years working Monday to Friday and never taking more than two days off in a row, who just snaps and burns out one day. Take time off so that you can come back at a higher level.

What the Owner Mindset Can Do for You

Again, our practice has been profitable through the Great Recession. It's been profitable through the COVID-19 pandemic—and I wouldn't call myself the most skilled dentist in town. We do take our craft very seriously, but the reason that we are one of the most popular practices in our area is because of the way we treat people. It's also the way we build ourselves, the way we build our team, and the way we structure operations.

Those are the three things that we're talking about in this book. To be consistently profitable just means to get patients to the place where they're happy and they come back, where they're okay coming to the second floor of an older building, where they are willing to drive a farther distance to get to us. And that simply means building a relationship with them. That means leveraging all the dollars you have, all the time you have, and all the mental bandwidth you have to form solid relationships.

It's just like any other business. Dentistry is a relationship business, so regardless of your starting point, go back to your relationships, adopt the owner mindset, and leverage whichever resources you have. If you do those three things, then business will come.

Chapter Takeaways

- Don't be fancy schmancy. Don't try to keep up with the Joneses. Next time you need to purchase equipment, ask yourself whether it is a patient-facing thing they will care about.

- To be Nifty Thrifty, whenever you must spend money, ask yourself whether there's a cheaper or even free way to get the result you want.

- Think about which resources you have in terms of your time, your dollars, and your mental bandwidth. What do you have the most of and how can you leverage it to get the people who pay your bills in the door and happy?

Chapter 2:

Leadership

We all know people who are stuck in their ways. Are you one of them?

These are the dentists who refuse to learn new procedures. They're the ones who have never bought a TV for the ceiling of their practice. They're the ones who buy the same old equipment, even though there's a more efficient or cost-effective model out there. This is the opposite of being a good leader.

Last chapter, we talked about how being Nifty Thrifty is being good and skilled and using your resources well. What does leadership look like in the context of Nifty Thrifty dentistry? To me, it's all about the growth mindset. You're going to see me say growth mindset quite a few times during this book, so you'd better get used to it.

Having a growth mindset means you have the humility and the honesty to take a look at yourself and realize that you can improve. You can get better. That's really part of the Nifty side of being a Nifty Thrifty dentist.

You realize as a leader that the more you know, the less you have to rely on other people's advice. You realize as a leader that the way you currently do things isn't necessarily the best way they can possibly be done. You realize the technology you use today might not be the technology you use tomorrow. You understand that there are things you don't know yet that you can learn. You realize there are ways that you can make more money and be more successful as a dentist if you think outside the box and take the time to learn them. You commit to constantly leveling up your skills and the skills of your team.

You commit not only to being a better clinician as a dentist but also to being a better businessperson. You treat yourself as one of your staff members who is on a compensation model. We'll talk more about what compensation means when we talk about our teams, but what I mean here is that I have all my staff members on a model where their pay scale advances with the skills they learn. In other words, the more they learn, the more they earn. Having a growth mindset means treating yourself the same way, even though you don't have to.

The other aspects of leadership involve determining your core values and leading by example. We'll talk through those as well, but first I want to home in on the growth mindset.

The Growth Mindset

Nifty Thrifty leadership involves consistent growth in three areas. These are your office, your home, and yourself. Obviously, growth in your office is huge. That's probably why you picked up this book. This means growing your clinical skills, setting policies that encourage growth in your practice, growing your patient base, growing your ability to retain your patient base, and finally, learning new skills to be able to offer higher-level treatments and reach a broader number of people.

But having a growth mindset also means growing your leadership in your home. What does that have to do with your business? *Everything.* You need to be the kind of dentist in your personal life that you are in your professional life. This way, your home life is in harmony and balance, and you can show up to work feeling fulfilled and happy. If you put on one persona at home and another persona in the office, it's going to wear away at you.

Lastly, it looks like a growth mindset in yourself personally. It means growing your skills, never assuming you have all the answers, and realizing that everybody in your life can teach you something—but also having the shrewdness to understand that not everyone has your best interests in mind.

Nifty Thrifty leadership is all about holistic growth. All three areas of your life need to be aligned and firing on all cylinders. In a word, keep an open mind and never stop growing.

Core Values

What do I mean by core values? I mean the kind of things that many businesses, including dental practices, plaster all over their walls, but never live out. Integrity. Growth. Unity. Discipline. Responsibility. Thrive. Whatever resonates with you, it needs to stop being something you just put on the wall and start being something that you live out in your everyday life. Again, not only at the practice but also in your home and your private life.

Do you have core values at the office? Is there a dusty poster somewhere on your wall espousing what's supposed to matter most? Are they something you talk about with your team, maybe once in a blue moon, but have no bearing on how the practice actually operates? If that's you, you need to take a step back and make sure that your policies and your day-to-day business really truly align with those core values. And once again, make sure they also align with your home and personal values.

That's where other dentists might get tripped up. Do you have values for your home and your personal life? If you have amazing values for your dental practice that help it be more successful and grow, why wouldn't you do the same thing for your household? Why don't you do the same thing for yourself?

Let me share some of my core values in the hope that it might inspire you to develop some for yourself. My core values are an acronym, FAITH.

Family
Awesome
Inspire
Team
Happy

Family is, first and foremost, the most important thing in my life. Everything I do in my practice and in my home is based on the family component. I treat my family the same way I treat my team. I treat my team like they are my family. And let's be real, I treat them like I would a good family member, not a bad family member whom I might avoid at Thanksgiving. I also treat my patients that way.

Awesome means going the next step or going the extra mile. I'm a child of the '80s, so the word "awesome" has always been part of my personal lexicon. For example, if I want to take my team to an event, like a continuing education (CE) event, I try to take them to something they'll always remember. I try to go over the top—something they'll talk about at the office and reflect on for years to come. We go over the top and above and beyond in everything we do. This even goes for things like cleanliness. My team isn't just cleaning the office, but we're scrutinizing the floor to see whether there's even a speck out of place and putting that in the trash. Why? Because again, we're awesome. We go above and beyond.

I is for inspire. We don't view our patients as just a tooth we fix. We want them to become better. We want their entire life to improve—even through something as small as dental health. If someone can manage their dental health well, it actually bleeds over, no pun intended, into other areas of their life. Plus, I try to inspire my team and my family to become better. I let them inspire me. It goes back to our growth mindset. Everything we do has a huge purpose behind it. I try to remind myself and my team of that every chance I can.

T is for team. Everything we do requires partnerships with other people. Every patient we serve, we serve as a team. I can't fix a patient's teeth without the help of my team. Even the relationship I have with the patients is that of teamwork. Because I know that if they don't take care of their teeth, they're just going to end up seeing me again, and maybe even in a worse state. So, we work together toward a common goal, their health.

Finally, we have happy. I want everyone to be happy. I want them to be happy at home and I want them to be happy at work. If someone isn't happy, whether it's a patient or a team member or one of my children, I always ask them, "What can we do to make you happy?" And sometimes, for a team member to be happy, they need to leave. Sometimes happiness for a patient means they need to leave, and we understand that. We know that none of the core values that I've talked about in the rest of this acronym will work unless somebody is happy. If you're miserable, you can't treat someone like family. You can't be awesome. You can't inspire, and you can't be a team player. So we do what we can to make everybody in our life happy.

I also have personal values and household values. I stay true to God, true to my family, and true to myself (in that order). What I mean by being true to them is to put them at the top. This doesn't just mean people in my blood-related family, but also those close to me. I try to treat them as more important than myself, and I try to maintain these values no matter where I am.

It's very relaxing when I realize I don't have to be a different person at home or at work or with my wife or alone. For example, if I try to scam people at work and then try to be a great dad at home, it creates a conflict. There's a dissonance between who I am in these contexts.

So, dust off the poster. Examine your core values, and don't just stop at your dental practice.

Lead by Example

Lastly, leading by example means that we take everything we've talked about so far and *apply it to our lives*. Many times we like to talk a big game about our core values or even our growth mindset and then our actions don't actually reflect it.

You have to realize that in everything you do, people are watching you. Your patients are watching you. Your team members are watching you—your spouse, your children, everybody's watching you. So you need to do what you say you will do. A lot of times bad leaders will say, "Do what I say, not what I do." That's the opposite of leading by example.

Can you lead yourself? Can you lead your office? Can you lead your home? And can everybody who's watching you say they respect you, that you do what you say you will do? That's what it means to lead by example. You're consistent. You don't need to put on one mask at home and another one at work. You don't need to be misaligned.

It means having integrity. It means that you keep your word. You tell the truth. You live out your core values in your office. If you gave everyone on your team a survey and asked them anonymously whether you stick to your core values, they would say, "Yes." And you would get the same result if you gave that survey to the members of your family.

Perform a Self-Audit

It's time to ask yourself some important questions. Nobody's grading you. Nobody's looking over your shoulder, but I want you to give honest answers to these questions.

1. Do you have a growth mindset? More specifically, if a new technology came along that promised to make your life easier, but it required some upfront investment either in your time or your money—or both—would you take that opportunity, or would you say, "Uh, you know what, it's probably not worth it"?

2. Do you have core values? Can you honestly say to me that the words you put up on a poster on the wall are also the things that you live by in your practice? Do you have core values that reflect the way you act around your family and home? Do you have core values that reflect the way you act even when nobody's around and watching you?

3. Are you leading by example? Can you confidently tell me that the person who shows up to your office, the person who shows up when you get home in the evening, and the person you are when the rest of your family is out of town for the weekend are the same person?

Chapter Takeaways

- Perform the self-audit, and identify any area in which you might be lacking.
- Develop a quick plan to start moving in the right direction.
- Make a special commitment to show up the same way you do to your home and your office.

Chapter 3:

Skills

I n the hit 2008 movie *Taken*, actor Liam Neeson famously declared to the criminals who had kidnapped his daughter, among other things, "I don't know who you are. I don't know what you want. If you are looking for ransom, I can tell you I don't have money. But what I do have are a very particular set of skills, skills I have acquired over a very long career. Skills that make me a nightmare for people like you. If you let my daughter go now, that'll be the end of it. I will not look for you, I will not pursue you. But if you don't, I will look for you, I will find you, and I will kill you."

I'm guessing your current skill set is slightly different from that of Neeson's character, but what I am sure about is that you do have a particular set of skills that you've acquired over your life. That's great.

What are your top skills? Write them down.

You might think, "Well, I'm not very good at that much," but that's not true. Usually people don't even realize the skills they have. They think a new thing is difficult because "I'm not good at learning new things," and then they do something they're more used to and think, "Well, that doesn't count because it comes naturally to me."

Why it comes naturally to you is because you've done it a thousand times! That's what I mean when I say you have skills.

Becoming a Nifty Thrifty dentist who works on themselves requires moving into the owner mindset, developing your leadership, and now developing your skills. You can think of it this way: Your owner mindset is the way you think. Your leadership is how you influence others. Your skills are the things you do.

We're going to talk about the three main levels of skills and the three main categories of skills. The main thing I want you to take away from this section is that skill acquisition has nothing to do with time and everything to do with repetition.

It also has little to do with natural talent. You can learn new skills if you adopt the growth mindset and take ownership of your development. Are you ready?

The Three Levels of Skill

I like to say that there are levels to this game. Much in the same way we have different levels of skill.

There are new skills, there are refined or upgraded skills, and there are skills you have mastered. And whenever you learn a new skill, you can move along the levels of mastery through repetition. It doesn't matter how long you've been practicing the skill. What matters is that you have intentional repetitions, practicing it over and over.

1. New Skills

A new skill is something you've just acquired. Every time you do it, you might learn something new about it. You still feel self-conscious and a little bit awkward when you perform it. Maybe you need somebody to go back and check over your work after you're done. Maybe you rely on an instructor.

There might be trial and error and mistakes you correct. You could run into situations where you're not sure what to do. It takes conscious thought and deliberation to perform this task. It might be frustrating, it might be fun, or it might be a mix of the two, but you start setting the foundation for the skill.

2. Refined and Upgraded Skills

Once you have started practicing the skill for a while, you start to feel more comfortable doing it. Even though you have a relative amount of comfort performing this task, you still figure out new ways to do it or ways to get more efficient at it as you go. The skill doesn't feel foreign. You feel confident understanding how to do it and perhaps even explaining it to somebody else.

But you still might use a little bit of conscious effort when you execute it. However, you notice yourself slowly getting more fluid and making fewer errors over time. Also, instead of thinking about what you're doing right now, you're also thinking about the next step. You're able to anticipate the outcome and adjust your actions accordingly. This is like a chess player who stops reacting to the other player's moves and starts operating out of their own sense of strategy.

3. Mastered Skills

A mastered skill is something that becomes second nature. This is a thing you can do in your sleep. It's something that you've done so many times that you can perform it without really thinking about it. You have a deep understanding and a new sense of intuition about it. You almost never make a mistake.

You might even find new ways to innovate and do the task faster that haven't really been discovered or thought about before. This is where you move from ease into artistry.

It's all about the reps. How is somebody who's relatively young able to become a leader who might surpass somebody who has practiced longer? It's all about the reps. I don't care about your age as a dentist. I don't care about how long you've been practicing. I care about how you're implementing what you're learning.

I would say skills are 20 percent learning and 80 percent application. It's more about the journey than it is about the destination. This requires an intentional decision from you to start putting in more repetition. What skill do you need to learn in your dental practice right now? What skill do you need to learn in your family and home life?

What's a personal skill that will benefit you when no one else is around? I need you to slowly but surely put yourself into situations where you're getting more repetitions. Move toward mastery in these skills. Go into uncharted waters. Even if you feel awkward or foolish at first because it's a new skill, it'll benefit you if you want to become a Nifty Thrifty dentist. You'll start moving into those uncharted waters and moving as many skills as you can from "new" to "refined" to "mastered."

Three Categories of Skill

Here are the three main categories of skill:

1. Clinical Skills

Clinical skills are the skills that pay the bills. These are skills you might learn through continuing education or at a special school.

You might learn a new procedure, a new way to manage your team, or a new way to perform something that you've been doing since the beginning of your dental career. These skills are huge for dentists because we need to provide the latest and greatest in terms of technology and care to our patients.

If you don't do this, you will eventually fall behind and other dental practices who have a growth mindset will surpass you in your clinical skills. And clinical skills are a massive part of what keeps your patients happy and coming back to you. It's also the ability to pick up specialized clinical skills like implants, ortho, endo, you name it.

The more services you're able to offer as a dental practice, the more successful you could become. Make sure that you are always in a mindset of refining and growing and mastering the clinical skills you have now and always be asking yourself what clinical skills you can adopt to help your practice the most in the years to come. Also, don't let the skills that you've already mastered collect dust.

2. Leadership Skills

We talked about leadership skills a little bit in the last chapter. In fact, everything we discussed in the last chapter is a skill, in a sense. The cool part about being a Nifty Thrifty dentist is you don't get to say, "Some people are born perfect leaders and I'll never attain their level." You actually get to learn how to become a better leader!

Let me prove it to you: The fact that you picked up this book is evidence that demonstrates your desire to become a better leader. The fact that you can understand the words I'm sharing on this page is evidence that you can grow and learn. So if you haven't already, do the audit that I talked about regarding your growth mindset, core values, and leading by example.

There are several domains of leadership in your practice and your home and personal life, so take a look at the areas you lack in and the areas you're good at, and intentionally refine both of them. These skills could include empathy. They could include casting vision. They could include having difficult conversations with team members or members of your family. Or it could involve your ability to teach other people. These are all leadership skills that must be developed over time.

3. Communication Skills

I put communication in its own category because it's one of the most critical skills you need to grow as both a practice owner and a leader.

One thing I love to do is learn and apply the love languages of the people in my life.

You may or may not be familiar with the book *The 5 Love Languages* by Dr. Gary Chapman. The five love languages are words of affirmation, acts of service, gifts, touch, and quality time. What I love to do is make sure I know the top love languages of everybody in my life and apply them consistently.

For example, if I have a team member whose love language is words of affirmation, I intentionally give them such words on a consistent basis. If I have a child who responds better to gifts or responds better to physical touch, I make sure to act accordingly.

One good exercise could be to have everyone on your team take the love languages assessment and talk through what that could look like when applied to a dental practice. This will help you become a better communicator because you'll be able to make sure the people around you feel loved by you and know that they can trust you.

Constant Improvement

Lastly, I want to share that just like with the owner mindset and leadership, developing skills is not a one-time effort. This is something that Nifty Thrifty dentists constantly improve on.

The growth mindset, in fact, dictates that you're constantly looking for ways to get better. You don't just focus on your internal life or your mindset but also focus on the things you can do in your world externally to make your dental practice or your family better. For me, this often looks like learning new things through books and audiobooks.

Nifty Thrifty Tip:

For every book I listen to, I ask an AI app to create a study guide for me to solidify the material. This challenges me to pay attention as I listen and figure out ways to apply what I'm learning to my real life.

As a Nifty Thrifty dentist, I encourage you to foster a lifelong commitment to learning and enhancing your skills.

Take a look at the areas we've talked about: our clinical skills, leadership skills, and communication skills. Make sure that you remain up to date with the latest techniques, technologies, and research in the world of dentistry so you can take care of your patients well. Make sure that you're doing what it takes to lead your practice well. Give the best possible experience to your patients and to your team members. Lastly, make sure you're learning how to communicate well.

Many of the problems that you'll face as a dentist are actually relationship issues when you boil them down. And what is a relationship issue but a communication issue? Make sure you know how to communicate well and how to make the people around you in your life feel loved. This will springboard your leadership and the harmony of your practice and family like none other.

The Secret Is in the Execution, Not the Education

If there's one thing I want you to remember when it comes to CE and other training, it's that your return on investment (ROI) doesn't come from the education but from the execution. This is really the secret to becoming a successful entrepreneur in any industry. It's all about execution.

Everyone has a good idea, and it's easier than ever to learn new skills at any given time. However, that's not what makes you successful, especially in dentistry. What separates the successful people from the others is execution. The successful people actually get things done. Skill upleveling isn't going to do you much good *unless you apply it*. Learning how to place an implant won't make you money. *Placing* an implant will. That's the difference.

Chapter Takeaways

- Determine which area—clinical skills, leadership skills, or communication skills—needs the most work.
- Identify one specific skill in that category you want to improve.
- Structure your next week to give yourself a plethora of reps.

Chapter 4:

Personal Growth

Unfortunately, I've known many dentists who were wildly successful in business. No, that's not a typo. You read that correctly. It was very unfortunate that these particular dentists made tons of money and had a wildly successful dental practice. Why? *Because it ended up destroying their personal lives.*

This is why I want to talk about personal growth and why it's so near and dear to my heart. It is one thing to be a good leader who has solid skills and who operates like an owner. It is another thing to have all that and not let the journey to success, or the success itself, destroy you. In fact, one of the greatest challenges facing the dental industry right now isn't the challenge of making a bunch of money and becoming successful; it's the challenge of staying sane, and of thriving.

We need to focus on ourselves so we can handle the success that comes from being Nifty Thrifty dentists. I'm not excluded from this.

Many dental books I've seen and people in the CE world often focus on the business. How can I be a better leader? How can I make more money? I would urge you to say that personal growth is more important.

How can you make yourself healthier? How can you be there for your family more? What really matters to you? For this, I like to encourage people to take a step back and ask themselves, "Why am I even building the business?"

What are you doing all this for? Why did you become a dentist? What do you want? What do you *not* have in your life that being a successful dentist will give you? What matters to you? And for you, maybe it isn't family. Maybe it isn't faith. That's okay. But *something* must matter to you. And so, as you build your business, you need to make sure you're focusing on and paying attention to the personal side of it as well because your personal and family fulfillment is just as important as—if not more important than—a successful business.

It's like the proverb of somebody who gains the whole world but loses their soul in the process. Make sure you spend time on what really matters.

Personal Growth Is the Engine

I liken personal growth to a car.

Think of it this way: Your business is an external thing that people see. They see you as Dr. so-and-so. That's like the paint job or the rims on a car. What is powering your business? What enables your team and you to take care of patients well? What's at the center of your family making sure that everybody is thriving? It's *you*. You're the engine. Your personal growth is the engine.

Without it, the car wouldn't move. If your engine breaks down, it doesn't matter how beautiful your paint job is. It doesn't matter what people see on the outside. It's not going to go anywhere. Similarly, if a dental practice owner breaks down, it doesn't matter how strong their team is. It doesn't matter how good of a leader they were before that. It doesn't matter how many specialized procedures they know how to perform. Their practice will begin to break down.

You need to put first things first and make sure the engine is always strong and healthy.

Three Aspects of Personal Growth

There are three aspects of personal growth. Notice how often I split concepts into three categories! It's for a reason. Putting things in these small groups will help you remember them better. Anyway, let's keep going:

1. The Physical

The physical aspects mostly come down to exercise and nutrition.

A. Exercise

Dentists have demanding schedules and require precision tasks that take a toll on their body. Therefore, every dentist can greatly benefit from consistent exercise. Not only will it help their physical endurance and hand-eye coordination, but it will also unlock so many mental benefits. We have a stressful job. Exercising consistently will help us maintain focus, regulate our emotions, and even give us better sleep. This will amount to better decisions in our dental practice, and also help us remain healthy for the long haul.

So I urge you to incorporate exercise into your daily routine. This could be weightlifting. It could be cardio. It could be a sport like boxing or even pickleball. Do something in terms of physical exercise that will improve your lifestyle.

Nifty Thrifty Tip:

If you incorporate physical activity into your everyday routine, it will make every other aspect of your life easier.

B. Nutrition

Second, on top of exercise, we need proper nutrition. Sorry to sound like I'm lecturing you here, but I'm sharing these things because they are so vital. What you eat will affect the way you think. It will affect whether or not you feel brain fog when you're doing your seventh appointment of the day, and it'll make sure you feel alert and make good decisions.

Think of nutrition as fine-tuning your engine. It has to go hand in hand with physical exercise if you want to get the most out of your body.

2. The Mental

We talked about skills and leadership in previous chapters, so that's not what I'm talking about here. This is a little bit different. You should intentionally engage in activities that grow your mental aspect that have nothing to do with your business or skills.

This could look like listening to audiobooks or reading books. You could read about philosophy or personal growth or history. It could look like journaling. It could look like solving puzzles—things that keep your mind sharp and give you a deeper understanding of yourself and the world. These things don't necessarily equate to making an additional million dollars this year.

So why do them? Because you need to have important hobbies that stimulate your brain outside the world of dentistry— or you will burn out.

3. The Spiritual

Lastly, attending to my spiritual beliefs is something that I find extremely beneficial, and many other dentists in my sphere do as well, so I couldn't leave it out. There must be a purpose beyond just getting up every day, performing dentistry, going home, and repeating the process, regardless of your religion or beliefs. We all serve a purpose and meaning bigger than ourselves. Otherwise, we simply wouldn't get out of bed in the morning.

Therefore, we all have some kind of spiritual aspect to us. So, I would encourage you to nurture that. We need an anchor that runs deeper than the cares of the present moment or the challenges of the day that enables us to not only overcome the challenges in front of us, but to do so with empathy, patience, compassion, and love. So whatever that is for you, I encourage you to treat the spiritual aspects seriously as a vital component of your personal growth.

For me, my walk in the Christian faith has been instrumental in shaping both my personal and professional lives. It gives me a purpose far beyond the ins and outs of the practice's day, and it enables me to connect with my patients, my team, and my family with genuine care, empathy, and love. It humbles me to realize how far I fall short of the glory of God and yet how forgiving and gracious God and the people in my life are. This influences everything I do as a dentist and as a man. It goes to show that your spiritual aspect will influence everything you do. So you had better pay attention to it if you want to be a Nifty Thrifty dentist.

Does this mean you need to adopt the same religion as me and do everything I do? No, I'm not trying to convert you. Instead, what I'm trying to say is that whatever spirituality looks like for you, embrace it and make a place for it in your life.

Efficient Ways to Grow Personally

I hope I've made the case for you of why you need to grow personally and some of the main categories you need to look at. Now I want to talk about efficient ways you can spearhead and supercharge your personal growth. Again, this ensures that not only will you become more successful as a Nifty Thrifty dentist, but you'll also be able to handle that success.

The last thing I want for you is to become a super successful dentist who can't handle it and ends up burning out while exploding your personal relationships. So, here are quick ways to start incorporating personal growth into your everyday life and business:

1. Adopt a Morning Routine

A morning routine that is consistent has tremendous benefits for you. It gives you a structured start to your day where you're always doing the same thing. This will set you off on the right foot, give you a positive tone for the day, and show you what you need to focus on. This ultimately leads to more productivity and also, in my experience, more enjoyment of the day.

It grounds me when I do the same thing every morning. It points me in the right direction and makes sure that instead of the day happening to me, I'm happening to it.

Here are a few things you might consider doing in your morning routine:

A. Spirituality, Meditation, or Deep Breathing

I personally love to focus the day by starting with prayer and reading scripture, but even if that's not your belief system, you can still benefit from meditation and deep breathing. Even just a few minutes spent meditating each day or reflecting on things that you're grateful for will help your focus and emotional regulation.

B. Physical Activity

As I mentioned, physical activity will benefit your life so much as a dentist. And so I recommend you find a small place for it every single day. This could look like doing a full workout or engaging in a quick session of stretching or yoga or playing a sport in the morning, like basketball or pickleball, whatever you need to do.

C. Healthy Breakfast

People have different opinions about whether you should eat breakfast or fast until the middle of the day. However, I didn't want to understate the value it can have, especially to dentists, when we don't always know when we're going to get a nice break in the middle of the day. Always starting off on the right foot in our nutrition at the beginning of the day can be a huge help.

D. Reading and Journaling

Reading and journaling can be great ways to start working on the mental aspect of your personal growth. Making a space for it every single morning ensures that it happens and that your mind is elevated beyond just the cares of that particular day. It could be reading a newspaper, reading a book, working on personal development, or even doing a crossword puzzle, but it will clear your mind. In my experience, it will also enrich your enjoyment of life, day in and day out!

E. Planning and Prioritizing

One thing I like to do as a dentist is review everything I have going on that day and ask myself how I can win at that. I like to visualize where I'm going to be, what challenges I'm going to face, and what things I might enjoy, and think through how I'm going to show up to those instances. This all helps a ton. It helps hard things be less hard, and it helps enjoyable things be more enjoyable.

2. Gratitude

Gratitude in itself has amazing benefits for your health and life that we're only just starting to research and study. It makes people more emotionally resilient. It improves their mood. It even potentially can lengthen your life and improve the health of your heart.[3]

So, beyond just doing gratitude in your morning routine, I also want to talk about it here. Find a place of gratitude in your day wherever you can, perhaps in multiple places. For me, one thing I like to do is reflect on things

---

3   VCU Health, "How Gratitude Can Help Your Heart," VCU Health, November 19, 2021, https://www.vcuhealth.org/news/how-gratitude-can-help-your-heart.

I'm grateful for at the beginning of each meal. This anchors me and makes sure I'm practicing gratitude consistently. After all, I always have to eat at some point, and practicing gratitude makes me feel so much better from day to day.

3. Goal Setting

One other thing for personal growth that you should do is set personal and professional goals. For example, you might have a goal about how much money you want to make in your practice, but do you have a goal about how much time you want to spend with your family?

I'll tell you what, your kids will not care how much money you were making while they were growing up if you weren't there for them. Thus, make sure that you set goals, not just for your practice but also for your family and for yourself so that your actions each day are aligned.

People mess this up. I often encounter dentists who say, "I want a $2 million practice without associates because I want more time for hobbies and my family." And then they wake up every day with a single-minded fixation on that $2 million practice. They don't care about anything else. They ignore their personal life. They treat patients like numbers. And one day they collapse, become miserable, lose all their friends and family, and burn out.

Now, I'm not saying that you can't have a $2 million practice and be happy and fulfilled at the same time. What I am saying is that you have to design your practice and your family life differently. It might mean adding associates, adjusting your fees, or targeting a different patient base. It might mean building slower and accelerating your business at a different pace than you would like.

Or maybe you want a $2 million practice, but you could actually get by with a $1.5 million practice that operates on a much better Nifty Thrifty budget and schedule.

Think about what you really want. Why do you want that $2 million practice? Is it because you want to spend more time with your family? Why not have a $1 million practice that gives you time with family, right here and now? Think through your true motivations; think through what you really want and why. That will enable you to set goals that align with not just your profession but also your family and your personal life.

I want you to succeed. I also want you to enjoy life while you're succeeding. Perhaps most importantly, I want you to get to the destination of your dreams and not have it destroy you. That's the importance of personal growth. And so I urge you to take a moment to think through areas that you could improve or little things you could do differently in this zone before moving on. Your life could depend on it!

Chapter Takeaways

- Think through the physical, mental, and spiritual aspects of personal growth. Is there an area that is weaker than the others that you could start working on today? Remember, you just need to start small and build from there.

- What does your morning routine look like? Do you rise at the same time every day? Do you do the same thing every morning?

- When you sit down to set goals, always have a why behind them. Ask yourself what you're missing now that you'll gain by achieving that goal. Sometimes we set big goals because it's what everyone's telling us to do or we don't realize that we already have what we're really looking for.

Chapter 5:

Shifting from the Operatory to the Boardroom

What does it mean to shift from the operatory to the boardroom? It means adopting the business owner mindset we talked about in chapter 1 and applying it to your dental business.

It means that as a dentist, everything you do has to make sense from a business viewpoint, not just from the viewpoint of a clinician or a leader of a team. This means mentally and emotionally separating yourself from the clinical side and the team side and thinking like a true business owner.

What if you were only investing in a dental business—you didn't actually work as part of it?

What kinds of decisions would you make about the kind of people you hire? About the kind of equipment you purchase? That's what it means to shift to the boardroom.

Think of yourself not as a dentist, but as an investor in a dental business.

This is because every dentist who owns their practice is a businessperson as well as a clinician. However, many dentists lack the knowledge or even the awareness that they need to treat their dental business as just that—a business. And so we need to begin mentally walking ourselves out of the operatory and into the boardroom of our dental business. This enables us to make strategic decisions to maximize our profit and reach our goals without getting bogged down by the fog of war that comes from being in the trenches as a clinician, day to day.

This is the main hat that dentists neglect.

The Three Hats Every Dentist Should Wear

Whether you realize it or not, you are three people in your dental business.

1. Owner, Investing in a Dental Business

As I just mentioned, your dental practice is more than just a place where you work. It's more than just a place where you do teeth. It is a business you're investing in. For many dentists, it is the only business they're investing in. It is their baby, their pride and joy, their nest egg, the thing they're going to retire off of. However, too many dentists see themselves as just clinicians, just practitioners of dentistry, instead of business investors in the world of dentistry. Do you see the difference?

2. Clinician, Doing the Work

Now, of course, we still have work to do from Monday to Friday. You also wear the hat of a clinician and a practitioner. However, almost no dentist I've ever met struggles with this hat. Everyone goes to dental school to learn how to do teeth; very few take the time to learn how to run a business. Still, there are operations to perform. So not only are you the owner of the business, but you're also the most valuable player in that business. So as you shift from the operatory to the boardroom, don't forget that you are your own most integral employee and you should treat yourself that way.

3. Leader, Managing a Team

Of course, no dentist is a one-person shop either. All of us have team members who help us, whether you have a small team consisting of a front desk person and a hygienist, or you're a multi-practice owner with dentists working underneath you. All of us as dentists are leading at least a couple of other people. That's the other hat we wear that we cannot ignore. Far too many dentists I've met have run into trouble because they are in the trenches doing teeth, but they neglect the human side. We're going to talk about our team mindset and setting up structures for everyone to win in the next sections.

Wear Your Owner Hat in the Boardroom

The boardroom is where you wear your owner hat. You can't neglect it in favor of the clinician hat or the team leader hat. Whenever there's a big decision to make, especially one that involves finances, ask yourself, "What would the best owner choose in this situation?"

This might be different from what a clinician would prefer. This might be where you follow the example I mentioned at the beginning of the book, where you invest in mid-level, but reupholstered, dental chairs instead of buying the top-of-the-line Mercedes-Benz of dental chairs. Why? Because that makes better sense from a business perspective, even though it may not appear that way from a clinical perspective.

Shifting from the operatory to the boardroom requires taking a step back, looking at the numbers, the cold, hard logic of every situation, and determining how you can reduce your expenses, increase your profit, and keep good people around. You're playing moneyball now. You're not just running a small amateur team that plays for the love of the game. You have an objective as the business owner to create, develop, and hold an asset that drives value for you and your family. Far from just a dental practitioner, you are an entrepreneur (whether you signed up for that or not). So it's best to embrace that and roll with it.

Example: Dental Products

Many times I see dentists trip up when it comes to ordering dental products. They want the top-of-the-line stuff, even if it makes no difference to the actual patient. So, one question every owner should ask themselves is, "What similar piece of equipment or product can give me the same or substantially similar results for less money?" For almost every product you buy, I guarantee there exists a less expensive, just as effective alternative that will do the job just fine.

This is especially true of equipment patients don't really see or interact with or know the difference about. These could be things like cotton swabs and gloves. I'm not saying you should skimp on wires, but I'm saying that for things that the patient can't even really tell the difference, see whether there's a less expensive alternative.

The problem is, we get stuck in a rut as clinicians. We get preferences. We start feeling loyal to specific brands. We don't take the time or spend the energy required to research whether there is a better alternative, and that would be all well and good—if we were just the clinician. However, those decisions don't make sense from a business standpoint. So again, take a step back from the dental chair and look at it from a different point of view.

What products are you using right now that can do the same job and give you the same results as something more expensive that you're currently using? What alternatives are out there? Take the time, even the next time you order, to start thinking through this.

In my time working with thousands of dentists to become Nifty Thrifty, I've found that this is the single greatest way to increase profitability for their practice. It isn't by adding more chairs. It isn't by going multi-practice. It is simply by doing the same amount of business as they're currently doing with less cost . . . but they can only get there if they stop thinking of themselves as a dentist and start thinking of themselves as an owner and investor in that business.

Wade Myers, GotaDental

How valuable is a good, trustworthy mechanic? If you think about it, you trust your mechanic with your life, especially if they work on your car's brakes. Having a good, trustworthy equipment consultant in your corner can feel the exact same way for dental practice owners when they shift their mindset from the operatory to the boardroom. That's where my friend Wade Myers from GotaDental comes in. He helps people make Nifty Thrifty decisions when it comes to purchasing, replacing, and repairing their equipment.

Wade is all about being nifty and thrifty. He wants to help people extend the life of their equipment, keep replacement costs down, understand all their options when it comes to purchasing new equipment, and find, source, and repair high-quality solutions, especially for dentists who are expanding, replacing, or upgrading their offices.

In a recent conversation, Wade told me that many practice owners don't really even know their options, especially when they're just starting out and they have a piece of equipment that feels worn or isn't operating the way it used to. They immediately think, "What new thing do I need to buy?"

However, Wade argues that for most pieces of equipment, you can actually find something that's been used and refurbished that'll function just as well for far less cost. In fact, Wade has built his business on helping people find high-end used dental equipment that can operate just the same, if not better, than new mid-level stuff.

We all know that when you buy a new car and drive it off the lot, its value depreciates significantly. The same goes for new dental equipment. However, that's good news if you are a Nifty Thrifty dentist because then you can look at newer equipment that's only been used for a year or two but has a significant depreciation in cost, even though it hasn't had a depreciation in function. That's the sweet spot.

For example, say there's a high-end dental chair one could get twenty years of use out of, but someone kept it for twelve years and now they want to get rid of it. You can get that dental chair at a significant discount and it still has seven or eight good years left in it. That keeps you from having to break the bank on a brand-new chair, and the patient won't even know the difference. They'll think, "Oh, this is a nice dental chair." It was high-end twelve years ago when it was purchased, and if you reupholster it, then boom, they won't even be able to tell that it's older.

This also frees up money for dentists to spend money in the right areas, like buying high-quality parts from an alternate supplier instead of the original equipment manufacturer.

One of Wade's crowning achievements was recently advising a doctor in Philadelphia. He needed a new compressor because the motor was wearing out. He was advised by a manufacturer that the new motor would cost him $4,500. Wade was able to take that $4,500 and get the dentist a used compressor with plenty of life left for the same price as the motor would have cost on his current one! See, with the right person in your corner, you can not only save money, but you can also get warranty protection on the refurbished or used equipment.

It's like going to a reputable smaller car dealership. They care about you. They want your business, and they'll stand behind the product because they can't afford not to. Whereas with a giant supplier, you're just another number.

Wade's piece of advice for dentists is to look at their equipment from the eye of an owner rather than a clinician who loves new toys. That's why having a trustworthy equipment consultant is a nonnegotiable for Nifty Thrifty dentists. And if you're curious about what Wade does or have a piece of equipment that you know needs replacing but don't want to break the bank, then go to GotaDentalLLC.com and get in touch.

Align Your Practice Ownership with Your Personal Goals

The thing I want to end on in this chapter is leaving you with the grand vision behind why you're doing dentistry in the first place. You aren't doing dentistry just to fix teeth. You're not doing dentistry just to help people maintain their dental health. Even though those are important things and worthy of doing all in themselves, you're also doing this because you have personal goals. You likely have a partner or family. You likely have plans to travel or have certain experiences. You likely have a desire to retire at a reasonable age and be able to live the retirement of your dreams.

The only problem is many dentists are operating as clinicians in the trenches. They aren't thinking about how what they're doing from day to day, week to week, month to month, year to year is getting them closer to their personal goals. They often hear they should want a practice that generates $2 million per year, or they hear that they should want to own multiple practices and be the head dentist among dentists.

However, they haven't stopped to think about their goal for themselves. I've noticed a divorce between people's ownership of a dental practice and their personal goals. In other words, they're just doing it because they're doing it, or they're doing it because they've been told by society or someone they heard at CE that this is what they should do.

Instead, dentists need to take a huge step back. Why do we need to shift from the operatory to the boardroom? It's because it allows us to see our dental practice as an asset we own. At the end of the day, your dental practice is ultimately an asset meant to generate and maintain wealth for you and your family. That wealth enables you to unlock a wealth of time and experiences, family time and leisure time. Your dental practice—every single aspect of it—should serve to get you to your personal goals. That's what I mean by alignment between your ownership and your personal goals.

I often use the example of having a practice that earns less money but gives a dentist more free time to spend with their family here and now, instead of a practice that uses up all the dentist's free time. Why is that important? Because if a dentist's personal goal is more family time, then they might be able to get that now with a smaller, but more efficient practice—rather than break their back to earn a bunch of money, to gain that time after their kids have grown up and moved out of the house!

So start thinking about what you want. When you have your personal goals for where you want to go in life—whether it's retirement goals, travel goals, family goals, you name it—then you can start to think of this tremendous, lovely asset you have known as a "dental practice" and use it as leverage toward your personal goals. If you fail to do that, you may get to the end of your dental career and realize that you wish you had spent more time with your family. Or more time golfing, or that you had been able to go and see Thailand, and you may realize that you don't have the time, money, or energy to do any of those things anymore. Or circumstances have shifted such that they are impossible now.

And I don't want that for you.

So I like to tell a dentist, "You can have a $2 million practice and a personal life. But it requires a shift."

You have to design your practice differently. You have to design your team differently. You have to design your fees, your costs, and your procedures all differently. You have to become nifty and thrifty.

You have the freedom and the power to begin thinking through what you want and using your dental practice to go after it. That's what it means to shift from the operatory to the boardroom.

Chapter Takeaways

- Every dentist who owns their practice wears three hats. They are a team leader, a clinician, and an owner. However, many dentists neglect their owner's hat.

- One of the biggest places this comes up is equipment purchases. Many dentists need to take a look at whether they can get less expensive but still functional equipment.

- When you zoom out all the way, your dental practice is an asset that can be leveraged toward your personal goals. Never lose sight of that.

Part 2:

Your Team

Chapter 6:

Team Mindset

Do you want to work a dead-end job? Do you want to show up every day to your job knowing you're going to be doing the same things day in and day out, week in and week out? All the while, knowing that your pay grade is almost never going to increase, knowing that this is it for you? Is that the kind of career you want to have?

If you answered no to any of those questions, then let me ask you this: Do you think your team wants that either?

Unfortunately, I see way too many dental practices set up dead-end jobs for their assistants, admins, and hygienists. And then these same dentists get surprised when good people leave! Plus, they have a hard time hiring new, good employees. There's a disconnect.

Thankfully, I know what the disconnect is. Remember in chapter 2, when we talked about growth mindset? All you have to do to find good team members is to take the same growth mindset you applied to yourself and apply it to your entire team. That's what it means to have a team growth mindset.

Think of it this way: The majority of people leave their jobs because they feel an incompatibility between themselves and their direct supervisor, whether that's a manager at a corporation or a dentist at a dental practice. They leave because they don't want to do the same thing all the time. They leave because they discover some other place they can go where they feel like they're growing, where they feel like they're going to get paid more, where they feel like their life's going to have more balance. And eventually, especially if they're superb employees, they leave, they go away toward that place.

So, our job as dentists is to think through how we can create an environment where team members with a growth mindset like us can thrive.

How Lack of a Team Growth Mindset Hurts

There are three primary ways that failing to instill a growth mindset culture in your business will hurt you.

1. Good People Leave

If you don't have a growth mindset in your team, you're going to end up creating dead-end jobs for all of your employees, perhaps even for yourself. Because no one wants to work in a dead-end job doing the same thing all the time, people will leave. Plus, the better an employee is, the faster they're going to leave.

Think of it this way: You have a rock star of a hygienist, and they know that they're one of the best. They're quickly going to realize it if they hit a ceiling in their career. It could be from a lack of pay raises, or a lack of opportunities to grow professionally. At this moment, they'll start looking for places where they can get paid more, places they can lead, places that give them more balance in their life and control over their schedule. They might look for places where they can start teaching new hygienists and have a team under them.

And they're going to realize this really quickly if you create a small pond for them because then they're a big fish in a small pond. If they're good enough to advance, but there's no advancement at your business for them, they're going to look to greener pastures.

2. It Costs You Money

In the long run, a lack of a good growth team mindset hurts you financially. This is because it costs money to hire. It also costs money to train people. Not only does it cost money, but it also costs time. If you have a new employee, their efficiency will be lower as they get onboarded into their new tasks. If you are constantly interviewing, calling people back, hiring them, and orienting them to their new job, it will rob you of time that could be spent generating revenue for your dental business.

So, when you have good people leaving constantly, it hurts your bottom line. It's one of those invisible expenses that you don't really feel until you've seen the other side of it.

3. You End up with Bad Hires

I'm sure that all of us can share stories about a team member we hired who ended up being a dud or even a nightmare. What's interesting is that we hired that person and we didn't think at the time, "Oh, they are going to be a terrible employee." That means there was a disconnect between our hiring process, our team, and the individual we hired.

After all, we are the business owners. We're the ones making the strategic decisions. We hired that person. We are responsible. And even if, on the off chance, you inherited a bad employee from a practice you took over, guess what? You're still their leader. You're still their direct supervisor. You're in charge of them.

All that to say, the lack of a team growth mindset really hurts when you begin getting consistently bad hires or your current employees start to sour because they don't have any way to advance their careers.

Hopefully, I've made the case now that you need a team growth mindset.

What Is a Team Growth Mindset?

Simply take the growth mindset you learned about in chapter 2 and apply it to your team. Only hire people who have growth mindsets. You know what a growth mindset looks like because you have one now. You've been listening to what I've been saying to you.

Then, teach your current employees to have growth mindsets. Tell them you want them to advance and succeed in their career. You want your dental practice to be aligned with their personal goals. Give them a runway, a ramp, a running lane where they know how to progress, how to advance in their career, and ultimately, how to make more money for themselves.

This means you must set up a structure that allows your employees to grow and get paid more because of it. "But wait," I hear you saying, "if I give my employees raises all the time, won't I be making less money?"

The answer is no. First of all, many dental practices are paying employees just to exist. If you think about the compensation structure at many practices, it really has to do with seniority and experience. This means that no matter how an employee performs, they'll get paid more simply by existing for long enough within that ecosystem. This is not a system that rewards high performers; it's a system that rewards people who can just stay in a rut and do the bare minimum day in and day out for years.

Second, I'm not saying you need to start paying your employees more because they're learning how to do useless things. I'm saying you need to pay your employees more when they learn things that make you more money as the dentist. You can set up your pay grades to align with new skills or key performance indicators that show that the employee is actually making the practice more revenue or substantially cutting down on costs. And therefore, the pay increase they get is just one small part of the net profit you've made.

How a Team Growth Mindset Solves These Problems

Thankfully, a team growth mindset has a direct answer for each of the three hurts we went over.

1. Good People Stay Longer

When you have a longer runway for your team members, then your good employees are going to stay for longer. That's Nifty Thrifty. You don't have to hire someone new every five minutes. It also means you don't have to hire someone with a ton of experience (who requires higher pay) because you have a runway for them to gain skills. You can hire fresher people based on their character and growth mindset, and then teach them the skills they need. This means these employees will cost you far less at the beginning of their career. But because they have a growth mindset, you'll be able to teach them what they need to succeed in your practice and make you more money.

Nifty Thrifty Tip:

Always hire for mindset over skill set.
The second one is much easier to train.

Remember, being Nifty Thrifty means spending money on what counts. What counts is the people. Your people are your most important asset. So what I like to do in my practice is hire people who have less experience in terms of the practical skills but have the right mindset and will be a great fit for our culture. This allows them to start at a lower pay grade, which matches their experience level—and then quickly learn new skills that help them become an even better asset to the team.

However, I say longer runway, not infinite runway. We all know that eventually people leave. Maybe they'll move somewhere. Maybe they'll get the job offer of their dreams. Maybe they'll decide a career in dentistry isn't their thing. Eventually, everyone does leave. The question is, have you gotten as much value out of them as an employee as they got out of you as an employer? Will they leave knowing they advanced in their career, learned skills, and can go off to something even better for them? And will you have them leave knowing they consistently made you more money year in and year out and had a great time while doing it?

2. Hiring and Training Is Easier

Now, if you only hire people who have a growth mind-set, it's a lot easier to train them. When you hire someone with little to no experience, you can train them in the skill sets that they need for your practice. They aren't stuck in habits of what they learned elsewhere in their career. They aren't coming in as prima donnas with certain demands or with ways they are used to things being done.

You also get to say to your new employees with a relative lack of skills, "Hey, this is the place where we grow. I don't expect you to be in the same spot by this time next year. I expect you to know new things. I expect you to be making more money." And you get to follow through on that promise. That makes the training process far easier because you instill clear motivation and create a running lane for your new hires to learn and grow. They can see exactly how much more they'll be making if they can learn how to do X, Y, or Z.

3. You Have Fewer Bad Hires

It's so important to learn to identify and adopt the growth mindset. Some people can learn to gain a growth mindset after having a fixed mindset. This is something you're going to have to try to do with your existing team members. It's something that you will have to do for yourself if you came into this book without a growth mindset.

However, once you do, it becomes a lot easier to identify others who already have that growth mindset. *Only hire these people.*

Think of it this way: If you look through the applications to your dental practice and find a bunch of people who don't have many skills yet, chances are most of them will newer in their careers and hungry to learn and grow. Those are the kinds of people you want to hire. More of those people are going to be growth-minded. Fewer of them will be set in their ways.

Then, you can incentivize them to leverage that growth mindset by structuring their pay grade a certain way. We're going to talk more about this in our next couple of chapters, but for now, I just want to explain how that team growth mindset has a cascading ripple effect throughout your entire business.

Don't Pay People Just to Exist

Again, if people don't level up their skills, then you're paying them just to exist in your practice. And at some point, if you're not leveling them up, then they're going to hit a plateau. And then you're going to end up overpaying them. That's not nifty or thrifty. We want all of our pay increases to be commensurate with the amount of money and value the team member is adding to the practice.

This goes back to the owner mindset. As a clinician or even as a team leader, we grow attached to people. We give them excuses. We cut them a break. As an owner, we see that not only is your employee a human being who is valuable and important, but they're also an asset to your business. And if you have an asset to your business that costs more money than it produces, you have a problem. Eventually, you won't have a business at all, and nobody will have a job.

You only get into that place, though, if you've refused to adopt the team growth mentality and give that person a clear runway to advance. Then you'll start paying them just to exist. You'll start overpaying them. You'll feel resentful toward them. They'll feel that resentment coming from you. They'll eventually leave—or create a toxic work environment that forces you to make that decision for them. I say all this very confidently because I've seen it happen time and time again.

Remember, it starts and ends with you. Having a team growth mindset means you need to have a growth mindset and maintain it all. Everything rises and falls on the leader of the dental practice, which is you. So revisit what I talked about in the chapter on growth mindset and determine whether you just skipped over it, or whether you've begun to internalize those values.

None of what I'm about to talk about for the rest of this book will matter one bit unless you have that mindset for yourself. Or worse, you'll learn how to develop an extremely profitable dental practice but have a terrible personal life and fail to reach your personal life goals. Either of those sounds like a terrible outcome.

On the flip side, the growth mindset tends to spread. When you show up to work every day with a growth mindset, ready to learn new skills, ready to grow as a leader, as a clinician, and as a practice owner, that'll begin to radiate out to your team members. Whether they realize it or not, your team members are looking to you for leadership. So lead them, lead them in a growth mindset, lead them toward learning new things and applying them to their jobs. As you get better every day, your team members will start to get better every day too. It'll have an exponential effect on your practice, and it can change your culture from night to day.

I promise you, the growth mindset will protect you, and your greatest asset, which is your people.

Chapter Takeaways

- When you have a fixed mindset as a team, it tends to lead to bad hires. It also tends to make good people leave your dental practice. It ultimately costs you money.
- When you have a team growth mindset, good people stay longer. You tend to make more money, and you have fewer bad hires.
- Before we dive into how to set up compensation structures for your team and train them well, revisit whether you have a growth mindset. None of this works without it!

Chapter 7:

Recruiting

Imagine something with me for a moment: You're interviewing an applicant for a dental hygienist position. Let's call him Earl. He seems to have all the right qualifications, although you're not 100 percent sure whether his heart is in the right place. Even so, you need to fill the position fast, and he's the most experienced out of your applicant pool. Plus, he's asking for less than some of the other candidates, so you choose him.

Now, imagine it's two weeks later. Morning arrives and you're opening up your practice. Your staff members make their way in, turn on all the lights, boot up all the equipment, and gear up for the day. You review your patient list and notice Earl has six patients he's seeing today. But you realize something: Earl's not here, and his first patient is scheduled to arrive in thirty minutes. You wait another ten minutes, and Earl is nowhere to be found. Your blood pressure starts hitting hypertensive levels and sweat starts beading on your forehead.

On the brink of panic, you call Earl, but he doesn't answer the first time. You call again; still no answer. Blood pressure is definitely high at this point. You call one more time, and he finally picks up. You ask him whether he knows he's working today, to which he responds in ignorance. He didn't know and didn't seem to care. You let him know that he has six patients today, but his response is less than passionate. He tells you that he'll be in as soon as possible, without specifying a time. You hang up, and your mind shoots back to the moment you hired him. It seemed okay at the time, but now, you're wondering whether Earl was the right fit after all.

Don't Hire an Earl

When it comes to recruiting your next superstars, you want to recruit the right people the first time. It is not nifty, and absolutely not thrifty, to constantly deal with staff turnover. You will lose more money having to hire and train new team members over anything else in your practice. It will cost infinitely more money, time, and heartache. Your staff overhead could be the biggest cost financially, mentally, and emotionally.

Think of it this way: If you don't have the right team members, you're making promises to patients you cannot keep. You'll find yourself trying to do everything, stretching yourself way too thin. This is not the path to nifty or thrifty. In short, don't hire an Earl.

Remember, the currency we pay to become nifty and thrifty includes more than just dollars in your pocket. It requires your mental bandwidth and emotional energy. When you hire the wrong person because you can get them $1 per hour cheaper, you might end up paying much more in terms of mental bandwidth and emotional energy, and those resources tend to slip away at an exponential rate. You can track how much money you lost, but you can never measure the consequences of losing energy or motivation.

The Two Pieces to Nifty Thrifty Recruiting

In our industry, we have three key currencies to look after: money, mental bandwidth, and emotional energy. Every hire impacts all three currencies, so never, ever recruit just on the dollars in your pocket. In fact, I would argue that the last two require more investment to gain than money, and I would definitely argue that the last two are more costly when lost over money. You can always make more money, but you can't always recover after losing the other two.

So, what does Nifty Thrifty recruiting look like on the ground, in a way that preserves and grows all three currencies? It comes down to two nonnegotiables: core values and culture.

Hire for Core Values

The best team members are the ones who share and believe in your core values, period.

In fact, there's a popular saying that claims "You hire and fire based on your core values." I agree. Those core values are the compass that guides every single human being. They dictate someone's mindset, integrity, follow-through, work ethic, and more in everything they do. It lies at the heart of who they are and how they'll show up for you.

Think of it this way: you can train someone in dentistry, but you can't train core values into them. Think of how exhausting it is to wear different masks at home or at work, trying to be a different person in different circumstances. It feels like you're walking barefoot on gravel. That's how it'll feel if you hire people who have to put on a mask to meld with your culture. It's unsustainable and *will* show up in the quality of your care.

Plus, when you make a promise to a patient, if you don't have the team members to follow through on that promise, you suddenly have an integrity issue on your hands. That's additional stress and strain that your practice does *not* need. Don't cut corners here.

Hire to Create a Culture

When you hire people whose core values align with yours, you're investing in your company's culture. When you're nifty and thrifty, your goal is to create a culture that's bigger than you and your business.

Without a company culture, employees work against each other and cut corners to grow. They feel like everyone's out for themselves, so they might as well focus on themselves and not the group, right? But when you've built a robust culture, everyone works together for the same goal: being Nifty Thrifty in all things. This is how you build a dentist practice that lasts.

How to Make Your Recruiting Nifty and Thrifty

1. Determine Their "Unteachables"

As Tony Robbins says, "Success leaves cues." When I'm interviewing someone, I look at two things: track record and actions. Their track record will be in their résumé, revealing what they've done in their career. Their actions will be observable by a rigorous application process, allowing you to take a peek into how they operate.

Our recruiting process involves discovering potential candidates' strengths, passions, and experience level. We focus on more than just hard skills—we make it a priority to figure out what we can't teach.

In your application process, you want to figure out those things as soon as possible. You can do this in several ways. For example, give detailed instructions that your applicant needs to follow before scheduling an interview. Ask them to prepare a résumé before an interview and send it over with a specific email subject line, in a specific format, or to a unique email address. See if they follow those unique instructions well.

Here's another idea for you: schedule a Zoom interview before an in-person one. Specify how the applicant must be dressed for the interview—for example, scrubs or professional dress. How well the applicant follows these details reveals how well they pay attention to details, which is foundational for what we do. This may sound unnecessary or even over the top, but trust me, this insight is worth its weight in gold and titanium implants.

2. Assess Their Personality

Let's say Applicant A's core values are right on the money. Awesome, but what about their personality? They must have the temperament to excel at patient fulfillment, intricate procedures, detailed bookkeeping, and more. Being exceptional at something is more than wanting to do it—you have to be wired in a way that allows you to grow, and grow quickly, in that line of work.

There are many ways to accurately gauge someone's personality. If you want to figure out whether Applicant A has the right personality for your opening position, here are a few tips:

Your applicants' interviews (Zoom or in-person) should reveal plenty about their personalities and temperaments, so you could stop there. But why not go further? As part of the interview process, ask the applicants to take a personality test, like the Kolbe assessment, Myers-Briggs test, or another one.

Have them imagine a stressful or complicated situation at work, then ask (in detail, of course) how they would respond to that situation. You'll discover swaths of valuable insight about that person in how they receive, process, and respond to those hypothetical scenarios.

You can also try a working interview with team members in addition to a solo interview, just to confirm that you and your team members are seeing the same things.

The whole idea is to have a rock-solid, colored-in picture of your applicant's personality. This is *not* an area where you want to leave anything to chance. Do your homework, then make your applicants do *their* homework too.

3. Evaluate Their Track Record

After you've determined that their core values and personality are excellent fits, you need to assess their track record. This reveals so much about the types of decisions they make, as well as the reasons behind them. Their track record demonstrates how the applicant carries themself in a variety of situations.

So, when interviewing an applicant, ask questions like "What's a tough situation you faced in your career, and how did you handle it?" "If I were to assign this task to you right now, what exactly would you do? What if X, Y, or Z happened all of a sudden while you were trying to complete that task?"

If they made a dramatic move in their career, ask them why they did it and what they learned from it. How are they implementing that lesson in their work today? Gauge how they absorb and execute information.

I also highly recommend bringing people in on a ninety-day trial period so you can see them in the office. During this time, observe whether their actions are in alignment with what they say. Start slowly and take your time to find the right people.

In all my years of dentistry and hiring, I've learned the hard way that you can figure out all of this and more just by reviewing someone's résumé and asking the right questions. If you don't, you won't figure it out, and you'll find yourself guessing more than you'd care to do.

One more thing: What if they don't have a track record? It certainly doesn't mean you can't hire them. If they seem like they have the right personality and share your practice's core values, then you can probably train them. This is a scenario where the trial period will be even more important. That way, if it doesn't work out, no sweat; you can move on. But if it does, you still had that peace of mind while you were feeling them out.

4. Don't Pay the "Hidden Premium"

Another reason recruiting the right people is so essential is that when you hire the wrong person, you'll quickly pay what I call the "hidden premium." You may have saved some money and time hiring Person A over Person B, but because Person A is grossly unqualified, they will make mistakes that will inevitably cost you the "hidden premium."

Don't fall for this. Imagine you're buying a new piece of equipment—don't skimp and buy the cheaper one. Bite the bullet and buy what will provide the absolute best value. You might as well pay the premium upfront instead of later when you weren't expecting it.

Here's the bottom line: Make the process rigorous to weed out the wrong fits. This is *your* Nifty Thrifty practice, so don't cut corners. Make every step count.

Chapter Takeaways

- It is not nifty, and absolutely not thrifty, to constantly deal with staff turnover. You will lose more money having to hire and train new team members over anything else in your practice. It will cost infinitely more money, time, and heartache. Your staff overhead could be the biggest cost financially, mentally, and emotionally.

- In your business, you have three currencies to look after: money, mental bandwidth, and emotional energy. Every hire impacts all three currencies, so never, ever recruit just on the dollars in your pocket.

- Hire for core values and to create a culture.

- Determine their "unteachables," assess their personality, evaluate their track record, and don't pay the "hidden premium."

Chapter 8:

Compensation

Imagine coming into your practice knowing that each team member is making exactly as much money as they want to make. Imagine knowing that the more money your team makes, the more money *you* make. Imagine your team members coming to you with ideas about how they could make *you* more money or free up more of *your* time.

When you build a Nifty Thrifty practice, that's not just a pipe dream. That's the plan.

If that's a possibility, why is it that so many practice owners feel like they are in a constant power struggle with their team?

Simple, because it's the way we've been trained to structure our team and payroll over decades. But just because it's how practices have always been run doesn't mean it's how practices *have* to be run.

In this chapter, I'm going to introduce you to a system that can make you excited to pay team members more because you know that the more they make, the more you make. This system can decrease turnover, push out poor performers while attracting high-performing team members, and more.

The beauty of the system is how simple it is. Not only is it simple to implement, but it's also simple to explain to your team. In its simplest form, people get paid more as they get better. But—and this is important—the system also includes a simple, clear path to getting better, so each team member not only understands how to get paid more, but they also know how to progress up the pay scale.

I call this compensation system a "Pay Grade System." Basically, I pay people to learn and implement (which is key) new skills in our practice. It's not enough to just *learn* skills—you have to *put them into practice and create value from them*. Here's what that looks like:

Pay Grade System

Like I said earlier, I don't pay people to just learn new skills. Anyone can do that in their spare time. Instead, I pay my employees to learn *and* implement. I'll help them level up and pay for CE and other training that will benefit both them and the practice. But they only get paid for implementing their new skill.

The more they learn, the more they can implement. The more they can implement, the more they can get paid.

Why? Because executing a skill well brings value (revenue) to our practice, so that person earns higher pay.

For example, I paid for my team to get laser certified. I didn't just pay for them to take a course or learn a new skill on its own. I compensated them to up their skill set and increase the value our practice can provide to our patients.

Now, they can offer a periodontal patient laser pocket reduction, a specialty procedure. Once they were able to implement that new skill and generate more income for the practice, they got more money. Simple as that. You get paid when you are actually using the skill, not learning the skill.

Or imagine if a patient comes in and needs an intra-oral scanner to check for cavities and other problems. If my people know how to provide that service, not only does it provide massive value (a.k.a. more revenue) for that patient, but it also frees up my time to meet with other patients, do outreach, or negotiate on the phone. Basically, if my people can execute more skill sets, I can delegate more responsibilities to them, which frees up my time to grow our practice. Everybody wins.

Growth Mindset

All of this comes down to having a growth mindset, particularly in dentistry. So many new team members come in, psyched to work in this industry and make a difference. But within a year, they feel stuck in a "dead-end job," unsure what happened between then and now.

Here's what happened: They lacked a growth mindset. They believed they learned everything they could within that first year, stopped learning, and lo and behold, they began to feel stuck. Here's the truth: As a team member, *you* are in control of your own destiny. If you want to learn new skills, you absolutely can and should. That's up to you.

That's why dentistry is not a "dead-end job." There are countless opportunities to grow and challenge yourself *if* you're willing to put in the work to learn and implement those new skills. If you're willing to grow, so will your compensation. It's that simple. You produce more by learning new skills, right? So in truth, your pay grade is largely determined by what you're willing to learn and do. There are other variables at play, of course, but you're more in control than you may think.

Why Pay Grade?

Imagine you have a team member named Nick. Nick has been serving your practice for almost three years, but he hasn't learned any new skills since he first started.

Nick's great at his same ol' same ol', but you can't ask him to do anything different because, according to him, he's not able to.

Then, as his third-year anniversary approaches, he begins asking for a raise. He *has* been here for three years after all, even though he hasn't done anything different since he first started.

Here's my question: Should he get paid more?

My answer: Absolutely not. Here's why.

Avoid the "Existence Tax"

Too many practices run into what I call the "existence tax." In essence, Nick's been here for three years; therefore, he should get paid more. Simple, right? But it's wrong. Nick hasn't earned higher pay just because he's worked here longer. In fact, I believe that this strategy disincentivizes your team members from learning new skills because, if they're going to get paid anyway, why not just cruise along?

Here's where I differ from the other guys: I believe people perform better, and are much more fulfilled, when they *earn* their raises and have a clear vision of their career growth. For beginners, this pay grade system encourages them to level up as soon as possible. For more seasoned team members, like Nick, they're motivated to keep things fresh and new, pushing past any limiting beliefs. Finally, novices are more incentivized to learn from experts, encouraging collective growth.

Remember, the workforce is no longer one where people stay in one company for decades. Nowadays, the workforce is much more transient and people are willing to jump around. This is why encouraging skill growth as often as possible is crucial to everyone's success.

The Four Levels of Pay Grade

In the military or government jobs, when someone hits a certain level in their position, they get paid more. This is because the military and government jobs both have a pay grade system in place that clarifies exactly what's required for their recruits or employees to get paid more.

You accomplish X, you move up to Level 2, and your pay increases to Y. Simple.

This is precisely why you need to link the skills they implement to your practice making more money—you must incentivize your team members to implement more and bring more value. It has to be skills that help you make more money.

At our practice, there are four levels for each position. Move up one rung of the ladder, and that person sees more on their paycheck. Go through all four, they have an opportunity to jump pay grades and into management.

Or a team member can get cross-trained, putting them on two different pay grades. They make more money because they are doing the job of two different people. No matter what your team members choose, the bottom line is that they can measure their progress.

Owner Compensation

This is what happens naturally for dentists too. For you to be able to make more money, you need to learn skills as well. Business skills. Clinical skills. Become more efficient. Maximize revenue while minimizing costs and overhead. In short, you'll make more as you become more nifty and thrifty.

Creating Your Pay Grade System

Everyone's pay grade system will be different, but here's a general guideline we follow to keep things simple:

1. Define the Levels for Each Position

Here's a general guideline to follow when defining your levels:

Level 1: Just came in off the street. They don't know much. Performing low-level tasks that people generally know without getting trained.

Level 2: They are performing all the tasks that need training for their position but still need significant supervision.

Level 3: They are able to perform a significant number of tasks with minimal supervision. They are also performing more complex tasks that take a lot of training to be able to do.

Level 4: They can operate minimally supervised and are performing tasks that are the highest level of complexity for their position.

2. Set the Wage Ranges

When someone comes in asking for $X per hour, I can go to my pay grade system and see whether they have the skills for that pay. If not, I encourage them and show them what it will take to get to the level. I let them know they will get paid to train to be able to perform more skills to rise up the pay grades.

Generally, I do a six-month performance review. Some people do annual performance reviews. Really, whatever works for you is fine. During these reviews, analyze what percentage of the skills needed to move up they can do. If they can do 50 percent of the skills, I give them 50 percent of the raise.

Here's the thing about wage ranges: You have to master the level before you move on to the next one. It's crucial that you're 100 percent comfortable with that level and its skill sets.

3. Have People Train Their Subordinates

Before they move up to a new level, they need to be able to train their subordinate at their previous level. As they say, the best way to master a skill is to teach it.

In many places, people are concerned about training their subordinates. But Nifty Thrifty core values always include a growth mindset, which gets reinforced with the pay grade system. So, no one needs to worry about being a good teacher—that will come naturally with the skill acquisition and training.

This pay grade system incentivizes people to teach. For example, let's say both Molly and Julie are at Level 1. Molly wants to level up to Level 2, so she's tasked with training Julie, a brand-new team member. Without this pay grade system, Molly could be wondering, "That's just more work for me. I'm already busy trying to level up to Level 2."

But with this system, Molly knows that an intrinsic part of leveling up *is* training Julie. This way, Molly is incentivized to do her best work, which benefits Julie. Plus, Molly gets the extra practice of training a colleague, which benefits her. At the end of it, Julie is a solid Level 1, and Molly has earned her Level 2. Molly led by example, and both practiced a growth mindset.

4. Establish Performance Reviews

I'm a huge believer in performance reviews. I believe measuring each team member's metrics is crucial to placing people in the right slots and ensuring their growth. Plus, you may discover untapped strengths in your team, which allows everyone to grow even faster and more sustainably.

Every practice is different, so every practice will need to design its own performance review system. If your practice doesn't know where to start or is itching to revamp your current system, here are some things to consider:

Generally, I do a six-month performance review. Now, some people will do an annual performance review, and that's fine too. You determine what frequency works for your practice. During that review, I see what they can do. And from there, it's basically a math problem.

Think about it: If a team member got 50 percent of the results and value we were aiming for, then they'll get 50 percent of that raise. If they got a quarter of the results, they would get a quarter of the raise. So on and so on.

Here's something I have to mention: I believe you will always get the biggest bang for your buck if you bring on someone with little to no experience. Why? Because you have a longer runway to work with in their pay. If you bring someone on who's at the top of the pay grade, you can't really go much further than that.

That's why filling up your docket with newbies is non-negotiable. Think of it like a football or basketball team: You have your stars who can't make any more than they currently do. If they want any more past your salary cap, they'll have to leave. Your rookies are there to fill in those gaps, and performance reviews keep that cycle running smoothly.

What If Someone Maxes out the Pay Grade?

There are several ways this can go, but here's what typically happens:

Imagine a dentist named Debra. Debra's been working with you for ten years. She's totally independent and can handle all Level 4 tasks. Combine that with her tenure, and she's capped out on your pay grade system. She's ready to move forward with her salary. What do you do?

Well, we could promote her to office manager, which is a viable option. However, Debra unfortunately doesn't have the managerial experience or skills to do it, and she would see that as a step back in her career. So, that isn't really an option. What now? Debra's looking to grow and doesn't want to stay capped. So, there's only one last solution: you promote her out of your practice to a better fit for what she's looking to do. Let me explain how this might work.

Sometimes, you can move someone into a managerial role and have them excel. That happens. But other times, as the leader of your practice, you have to determine whether someone is ready to move beyond your practice to another practice or even another business where their growth and structure better aligns with the team member's continued growth. It's never an easy decision to make, but it's sometimes the best path for both their career and your practice long term.

Remember, we only get paid for whatever we produce. We don't get paid for just showing up. Now, on the flip side, if there's someone who has the aptitude to become management material, then they go through another pay grade system, which depends on how your team is set up.

For example, it could be management and training, assistant manager, or office manager. It could be a treatment coordinator, insurance coordinator, or beyond. But once they get into the executive role, then they go through a different pay grade system as well. Plus, they develop certain new skill sets along the way. Again, the key to the pay grade is the new skill they're learning.

Chapter Takeaways

- A pay grade system incentivizes team members to learn and implement new skills to advance (and helps you avoid the "existence tax").
- Requiring team members to teach subordinates accelerates growth for both.
- Establish semiannual or annual performance reviews to maximize growth.
- If someone maxes out of your salary range, either promote them to manager or promote them out of your practice to continue their growth.

Chapter 9:

Training

If there's any NFL team that's defined history in Super Bowl wins, it's the New England Patriots. Between 2001 and 2019, they achieved something few teams ever taste in team sports—a record six championship victories in under twenty years. That's incredible, and it comes down to more than sheer talent or luck. It's training.

Imagine an NFL team: There are fifty-three men on the roster plus twelve on the practice squad. With that many guys running around, the potential for error is enormous. How do you get all the pieces to run well together?

The Patriots had plenty of talented and hardworking guys, but so what? Every NFL team does. What made the difference between them and their competitors? A little-known quarterback named Tom Brady.

Most people know that Tom Brady had an exceptional work ethic and was an excellent player, but that's not the only reason the Patriots won the Super Bowl six times. One crucial factor was how, during those eighteen years, Brady consistently took a pay cut to build a stronger team. That's right. Arguably the best QB in the league was getting paid *less* than he could have been.

Why did he do it? Because Brady was committed to making the Patriots truly great, no matter the cost. So, he cut his pay in order to set an example of self-sacrifice and dedicate himself to training his team.

Plus, Brady's example convinced some of his teammates (Randy Moss being one of them) to do the same. Over time, this created a culture of self-sacrifice for the greater good. The more players who did this, the more the whole team was committed to bringing everyone over the finish line.

Training in Dentistry

I'm not suggesting that you pay people less than they've earned. Not at all. Invest in your people and pay them well. However, here's my point: When everyone, including the owner, views their role as a key member of a team, money becomes only one measure of what's important to each person. Everyone starts to laser in on what truly matters.

Many teams don't sustain success for this very reason—they focus on money and rewarding themselves over the success of the whole team.

With dentistry, there's no contractual salary cap, but there's a reality salary cap. You can only spend so much on your team, so you have to field the best team you can. This means you have to constantly plan for team members to leave. This also means that you have to consistently recruit and train people to move up and fill in the gaps. Not everyone on your team will be the Tom Brady of dentistry, but when you invest in proper training (hard skills and soft skills), you'll quickly reap the reward: a team that cares about moving forward together.

This means that you can't just train people to train people. Your training needs to have a purpose imbued into it—a purpose greater than each person. There are countless reasons you can train your people, but in our industry, here's how we approach training:

Train People to Level Up

Remember how I talked about the various pay levels in chapter 8? I believe that training to learn new skills is crucial to leveling up. What does that look like?

First off, training your people means they get to move up the pay grade. As we discussed in the previous chapter about pay, you need to train your people to allow them to move up the pay grades. That training is all about teaching your employees new skills *and* how to implement them to bring more value.

Second, your training exists to prepare your people to assume more responsibility in your practice. Years ago, when anything went wrong, I was the person called in to solve the problem. While I'm still the one who puts out the big fires, I've trained my team on how to handle the smaller ones so I don't have to. When you approach your practice this way, everything will run far more smoothly.

For example, if you have a manager who's preparing to leave your practice, it's imperative that you train other interested team members to replace that manager. Not everyone is interested in leadership positions, but for those who are, your training is their stepping stone.

Train People to Train Others

In the Apple Montessori classrooms, it's common for older students to teach younger ones.[4] I believe we should approach our businesses the same way. In our practice, the veteran team members routinely assist and teach the less experienced ones, which ends up benefiting both of them over the long run. I'm a big believer that one of the most effective ways to learn something is to teach it, and that happens over and over again at our practice.

Ultimately, you're training others to replace you one day. That may sound morbid, but it's the truth. Remember Tom Brady? He was doing the exact same thing, knowing that he couldn't play forever. When you train your leaders to be teachers of your craft, you're investing into the longevity of your practice. Never forget that.

---

4   Apple Montessori, "What Is a Mixed-Age Classroom and How Does It Benefit Your Child?," Apple Montessori, n.d., https:// applemontessorischools.com/blog/what-is-a-mixed-age-classroom-and-how-does-it-benefit-your-child.

How to Train Your Team

Training your team is its own art, which is why it has its own section. When you train one person, you're dealing with one dynamic, one manner of doing things. With a team, you may have dozens of people, which means your approach should be more systematized. It comes down to meetings, milestones, and plans with clear goals. Here are some ideas.

Set Milestones

Nothing gives people more clarity and motivation than clearly defined goals, and setting milestones is an awesome way to do it. For example, if your goal is to train your entire team on all periodontal procedures, set a ninety-day plan with clear benchmarks to meet. Discuss this plan with your team, collectively and individually, to get everyone on the same page.

Set Up Regular Meetings

Next, set up regular meetings between team members and their team leaders. Consider semi-regular meetings with your leaders to figure out what kind of support (if any) each team member needs to meet that goal.

It doesn't matter if your team members start at different points—that's a given. What matters is that everyone finishes together—meeting that goal you set in the beginning.

Make Moving Up the Pay Grade Flexible

If you have a team member who's knocking everything out of the park, consider allowing them to move up the pay grade faster than the standard six-month or annual review period. If someone is ready to learn new skills and provide more value, don't let your framework constrain them. Train them to keep moving up the ladder and bringing more value. A key to training your people well is meeting them where they are, not where you expected them to be.

How to Get Buy-In from Your Team

After reading all of that, you might be wondering, "That all sounds fantastic in theory, Glenn, but how do I get buy-in from my team? How do I know they'll get on board with this idea?" Great question. Here's what I recommend.

Right off the bat, there's no guarantee of how your team will react. I don't know your team and won't be so bold as to suggest exactly how they will react. However, I firmly believe that if you bake your milestones into the fabric of your training, your team will be driven to learn and do more.

For example, I recommend you make training milestones an integral part of your pay grade system. That way, getting paid more means acquiring *and implementing* new skills. There's no separation; they're one and the same.

Moreover, require team members to train others before moving up the pay grade. Once again, you're incentivizing each member to invest in the success of their teammates, which is crucial to everyone's success.

The more you repeat these two steps, the more "bought-in" your team will feel with you and each other. A rising tide lifts all ships.

The Four Disciplines of Execution

If you're ready to add rocket fuel to your daily execution, here are the four principles by FranklinCovey that have worked wonders for our practice.

1. Focus on Your Wildly Important Goal

If you're training your team, don't just measure their success by production. Production is a lag measure, meaning two things. One, you can't measure it until after it's occurred. Two, it's too rigid of a metric with the constantly changing demands of your practice.

Instead, we love using what Covey calls your "Wildly Important Goal." Let's say your WIG is twenty-five new patients per month. Awesome. Don't just focus on that. Focus on the leading measures that will allow you to achieve your WIG: outreach, lead generation, word-of-mouth referrals, and so.

When you train your people, cultivate a culture that focuses on the lead measures like learning new skills, not just the WIG. That way, your team members (and you, for that matter) aren't losing sleep over whether your practice is making money or getting new clients. Everyone's focusing on what they can control, and it helps them know they're moving in the right direction.

2. Measure Progress by Lags and Leads

Measuring progress is necessary for making progress, and training your people works the same way. You need to measure progress (as a team and for each person) to ensure that your practice is moving forward.

However, "progress" doesn't only mean revenue, profit, or patient satisfaction. Those metrics are important, of course, but they aren't everything.

According to research by FranklinCovey, progress should be divided into two buckets: lag and lead measures. Lag measures are what I just listed, including revenue, profit, and customer satisfaction. They're called "lag" because, as FranklinCovey puts it, "By the time you see them, the performance that drove them has already passed." In other words, you only know you made a profit if you've already made a profit. You can't change it.

By contrast, there are other factors called lead measures. Think of it like weight loss. Weight loss is the lag measure, so what's the lead measure? A proper diet and exercise. Why? Because those two activities predict the likelihood of weight loss.

2. Keep a Compelling Scoreboard

Have you ever watched young kids play some sport without keeping score? To spare you the details, it's not terribly exciting or deliberate. Sure, the kids are having fun, but they quickly get bored. There's nothing keeping them accountable, so why play their best? Why play to win?

People play differently when they're keeping score, and the right kind of scoreboard motivates people to win. With a scoreboard, people are engaged. They're committed. They're dedicated and can see progress in real time. The best scoreboard is designed by and for the players, which means you and your staff. As you design yours, remember that your staff will be maximally engaged when they know whether they're reaching their goals or falling short.

3. Create a Cadence of Accountability

Accountability is foundational to success, no matter what industry you're in, but it's monumental in dentistry. This is where regularly scheduled meetings (whether daily, weekly, or even twice a month even, doesn't matter) are crucial to success: they maintain a cadence of checking in, making corrections, and connecting with your team. Each meeting is no more than twenty minutes because, let's be honest, no one likes long meetings. No one.

People are far more likely to commit to goals that they agreed to, not ones that came from on high. When they set a goal and reflect on their wins in those regular meetings, it's massively inspiring. In fact, when your team is accountable to each other (and not just you), it becomes more than just a company bottom line. It becomes a promise to themselves to succeed. That's turning the dial from four to eleven. When the team sees they are having a direct impact on the WIG, they know they're winning.

In my experience, nothing drives morale and engagement more than winning.

Training Tools

In my practice, every position in the practice is not just connected to the pay grade system but also the specific tasks they need to be able to do. Similar to a job description but in more depth, we begin with skills and then customize them for each team member. We want each team member to make as much money as possible.

This structure not only helps us get each team member to make more money, but it also helps us make sure each person is currently working.

Every position should have a training manual.

Use project management software such as Asana or Trello to track progress and keep a log of what they've completed, what resources they have available, and what they need to do to keep growing. Project management software also allows team members to communicate with you and each other to ask questions, request resources, or input milestones.

Include training, certifications, or skills needed. For example, we have an assistant who wants to go to hygiene school. She's at the top of the pay grade for her position, but we're putting her through coronal polishing training so she can expand beyond her specific pay grade system to earn even more money.

With her, she will eventually go to hygiene school and will need to earn this certificate anyway, but understanding her goals helped us customize training to allow her to make a small jump into another position's pay grade system that she wants to eventually get to without having to completely change positions. The coronal polishing training allows us to tie additional pay for her with additional value to the practice, even though it's technically beyond her position.

Chapter Takeaways

- Every team member should train others (mixed experience levels) to ascend the pay grade ladder—it creates a culture of learning and connection.
- Train your team with milestones and a flexible pay grade system.
- Implement the Four Disciplines of Execution (Wildly Important Goal, Lags and Leads, Compelling Scoreboard, and Cadence of Accountability).

Chapter 10:

Retention

I'm often approached at conferences by hygienists looking to advance in their careers. While the conversations have unique elements, the general point is pretty consistent. They love what they do and clearly know their stuff, but they tell me something is off.

I dig a little deeper (no pun intended), and they fill me in (pun intended) on the culture at their practice and learn it was not good at all.

Many times, these hygienists tell me how they want to learn new procedures and move up the ladder, but their practices don't offer training or pay incentives to learn. So, they spend hours after work studying books on their own time, hoping to eventually find another practice where they can use their new skills and get paid for it.

Some tell me about their coworkers taking breaks multiple times a day. Once they are done with their primary responsibilities, they stop working and take a break. Many of them would love to have something else to do to earn more money or learn new skills but the practice doesn't offer these opportunities so they just take a break. Others are just happy to do the bare minimum and take as many breaks as possible.

I'm no longer surprised by these conversations because they happen so frequently but I can never forget what they tell me. Here are these exceptional hygienists ready to do more and get paid for it, but they feel so stuck that they're just preparing to leave as soon as possible. Their coworkers seem to be doing the bare minimum, too. It all feels so wrong.

Then I talk with practice owners who tell me how hard it is to find and motivate team members, not realizing that they often already have motivated team members on their team. They just don't create opportunities for those team members to do their best work, so they are all preparing to find another job, leaving behind the team members who are happy to do the minimum and take breaks with their downtime.

This is how people feel "stuck in a dead-end job." People only think they're in a dead-end job if they think they can't grow. But in reality, there may be endless opportunities for growth that haven't been tapped into yet. Having a growth mindset changes all that, which opens the door to new opportunities across the practice.

Above all, feeling safe and appreciated is all about the owner and leaders knowing what's important to their staff, then acting on that information.

Work with What You Have

My goal in writing this book is *not* to create a one-size-fits-all guide that tries to apply to every practice. Spoiler alert: I couldn't do that even if I tried. Every practice starts from a unique place, employs unique people, and serves a unique audience. Basically, a practice in rural Texas shouldn't apply the same things a practice in suburban Chicago should. Different people, different circumstances, different goals.

Instead, this book can be summarized with the five words you see written above: *work with what you have.*

Use this book like those old Mad Libs books, filling in your particulars and fine-tuning it until you get it near perfect. In all honesty, this book isn't only for dentists. Whether you own an ice cream shop, a real estate company, or an Asian fusion restaurant, these concepts are universal and can be customized for your business.

In short, don't follow everything to a proverbial T. I'm giving you the blueprint, but it's your job to fill in the details.

Three Crucial Questions

Leveling up your retention comes down to asking each team member these three massively important questions. The insight you get will be priceless because, to a high degree of specificity, you'll know how they've felt up to this point, how they currently feel, and how they perceive their future. Every chapter in this book exists to answer those three gargantuan questions.

1. Do They Feel Appreciated?

Back in chapter 3, we discussed the five love languages and how important they are for understanding each team member. The sooner you understand the primary language for each person, the better you'll understand whether they feel appreciated. Plus, if there's a deficit to make up for, you'll know where to invest your energy so that they know you value them.

Here are the five love languages, listed in a way that we can use them in our context.

1. Words of Affirmation

For some folks, nothing makes their day quite like hearing "Awesome job, you really nailed that." This can look like complimenting their work, offering positive feedback for a procedure, or simply saying how much you appreciate them for the hard work they do every day. Don't complicate what you say or how you say it—just pay attention and acknowledge what you notice. It goes a long way.

2. Quality Time

You'd be amazed how much your team members appreciate a simple lunch invitation or one-on-one meeting with you. When you work with someone whose love language is quality time, nothing makes them feel more loved than knowing you're paying attention.

3. Gifts

At my practice, I know my team's favorite Starbucks drinks, candy flavors, Chick-fil-A orders, and more. How? Because we send out questionnaires regularly to pool all of that information. Why? Because I know a few key people on my team feel the love when they receive a gift of any kind. The more personalized, the better.

4. Acts of Service

This could mean helping a team member clean a room after a procedure, organizing a team volunteer event for a cause the employee is passionate about, or simply grabbing a toothbrush for that person when they're doing a patient cleaning. Whatever it is, they feel deeply loved when someone (especially their leader) helps them with everyday tasks.

5. Physical Touch

This one may sound the least applicable, but you'd be surprised at how a little can go a long way. For example, if Bill's love language is physical touch, give him a high five every time he finishes taking care of a patient. Throw him a fist bump every time he organizes his station or completes patient intake. Whatever it is, making that physical connection is what will make him feel seen and valued. Of course, be careful of using physical touch in the workplace to make sure any physical contact is appropriate, wanted, and appreciated—hence my high five and fist bump example.

2. Do They Feel Safe?

When we talk about vision, it circles back to this core idea. Every day when a team member comes in for work, do they have a path to success and possess the resources to move forward? Can they access the training and systems necessary to make progress?

In short, does the team member know they can build a future at your practice? That peace of mind influences so much in their professional journey, which inevitably rubs off on your practice as a whole. So, it's imperative that you create that feeling of safety for each team member. Moreover, it's crucial that you know what they value so that they feel safe to plant roots with you.

Practically speaking that looks like this: With each new skill they learn, they level up and move up the pay grade. They get closer to doing what's valuable to them. In short, they can see their future laid out in front of them, which creates that feeling of safety.

One tool I use with my team is to have them draw up a vision board for their future, so I can understand what motivates them. Understanding your team members' hopes and dreams is crucial to helping them feel safe and invested in.

3. Do They Have a Future Here?

How often have you heard something to the effect of "I feel like I'm stuck in a dead-end job?" Do you know why people say it? It's often because they genuinely don't feel like they can grow in the position they're in. They truly feel stuck. They don't want to stay in their position and pay grade. They want to move up but don't see a path to do so in your practice.

You can eliminate those concerns in each person, but trying to do that yourself (especially if you have a large team) requires unlimited bandwidth. It's not efficient, nor is it honestly that effective, Instead, this all comes back to culture. Does your entire practice (not just a few star players) *know* that they can build a future here with all the resources and encouragement they have available to them?

Fostering that culture comes down to three distinct steps that, when used in tandem, cultivate that culture of growing roots with your practice.

1. Pay Grade and Upward Mobility

I probably sound like a broken record at this point, but I can't highlight this point enough: your pay grade system must, and I repeat, must offer upward mobility in your staff.

For example, if a staff member is itching to learn coronal polishing (a.k.a. cleaning with fluoride), offer to pay for training so they can learn that skill. Then, once they start implementing that skill into their everyday practice, move them up the pay grade. From there, continue incentivizing them to expand that skill set or learn another one. Rinse and repeat. This is how you *show* (not just tell) upward mobility in your practice, which does wonders for your retention and culture as a whole.

If they bring more value, they get paid more. It's that simple, yet it's unbelievably powerful. Don't force your staff to imagine a future; create it for them.

2. Helping Your Staff Grow

In case you couldn't tell, this is a big one for me and my practice. People feel stagnant because they don't feel like they can grow, or they don't know whether it's possible. Even if you offer everything I've described up to this point, none of that will matter if your team members don't believe they can grow. If they believe they'll stay stuck, they're right. But if they scrap that thinking and adopt a mindset of growth and mobility, they'll finally be able to envision their future. Seeing that happen is one of the reasons I love what I do.

Also, team members only level up to the level of the leader. If you don't believe your practice can grow and grow fast, neither will your team. Set the standard and live by it, every single day.

3. Recruiting People with Growth Mindsets

In real estate investing, experienced investors will tell you "The money is made when you buy." In other words, when you buy the right property at the right price, you end up making a lot more money than if you buy the wrong property or pay too much, even if you invest a lot of time and money improving the "wrong" property or a buying property for which you paid too much.

The same is true with retention. It may sound like Hiring 101, but you have to recruit the right people. You have to recruit those who are willing to envision their future with you, who refuse to stay stagnant and are ready to move forward whenever possible. The more you do, the more those people influence the rest of your team. If an applicant isn't a slam-dunk in the mindset department, then they're not the right person for your practice. That standard is what has propelled us forward all these years.

You Can't Keep People Forever

In all my years as a dentist and business owner, one of the most bittersweet parts of my career is seeing incredible people leave my practice. It's never fun to do because we're losing a piece of the puzzle that feels irreplaceable. However, I'm also psyched for them because I know they've grown so much and will bring immeasurable value to their next position, or even to a practice of their own.

This brings me to the last point of this section: you *cannot* keep people forever. You just can't, and you probably shouldn't. If you're doing your job right (see the chapters before on how to), then that person will eventually outgrow your practice.

Maybe they hit your salary cap but are ready to keep climbing. Maybe they want to learn new skills that your practice doesn't offer. Whatever the reason, your job is ultimately to help them become the best professional they can be, not to keep them glued to your practice forever.

As a result, you'll undoubtedly have "that" conversation with many of your staff members over the years. That's okay. That's a good thing. Celebrate their achievements, give thanks for the value they've created, and send them on their way. You may feel the sting temporarily, but deep down, you'll feel this profound sense of accomplishment and fulfillment.

Chapter Takeaways

- People feel "stuck in a dead-end job" when they have no opportunities to grow, learn more, and get paid for it.

- This book is not a one-size-fits-all plan to tell every practice owner how much to pay people, what procedures to offer, whether to take insurance, and so forth. That wouldn't be helpful. It wouldn't work. It's a blueprint to take and fill in the details that match your vision, your goals, and your practice. It's designed to "teach you how to fish," as the old saying goes.

- To improve retention, answer three crucial questions: Do they feel appreciated? Do they feel safe? Do they have a future here?

- Recognize that you can't keep people forever if you do your job right—that's a good problem to have. It'll mean your team members are constantly improving and you will likely have a replacement ready internally.

Part 3:

Your Operations

Chapter 11:

Systems

In the mid-1980s, before e-commerce and online inventory management could revolutionize ordering, a creative dentist leveraged dental suppliers using a fax machine and a collaboration of dental practices to combine orders to get suppliers to bid on prices.

One of those suppliers, a nimble start-up called Crazy Dental Prices eventually found itself bidding on orders from all around the US. Today, Crazy Dental Prices is the marketing arm of DC Dental. They have a really cool story. They're local to the DC area but have grown nationwide and are using e-commerce and systems to grow their business.

Crazy Dental Prices didn't start out as a big company with unmatched systems, however. It started with a dentist and a vision: "Dentists need a direct partner for their supplies."

I sat down with Jay Glazer, Crazy Dental Prices' director of business development, to discuss their history and how they implemented industry-leading systems that allow them to compete with other companies around the world that are often bigger, better funded, or have other strategic advantages.

Jay refers to the early days of Crazy Dental Prices as the "Hotwire of Dentistry." At the time, Crazy Dental Prices was one of many companies bidding to fulfill orders from practices around the country. Over time, Crazy Dental Prices began winning a significant percentage of orders, fulfilling about half of all orders.

As time passed, Crazy Dental Prices found itself in a tough position, competing on price against other suppliers selling "gray market products." If the term is new to you, it basically refers to legitimate products purchased initially by overseas purchasers and then resold into the US.

As strange as it might sound, companies can save a lot of money by buying this way because manufacturers often sell to overseas groups at a lower price than they sell to US buyers because overseas buyers simply can't pay as much as US buyers can.

This practice was common in the industry and helped lower costs to practices, but it wasn't without risks. For example, it created an environment where a company could easily create knockoff goods that were lower quality and sell them to practices as if they were authentic.

One decade ago, Crazy Dental Prices decided to take on gray market suppliers and contacted the manufacturers directly to, in Jay's words, create an arrangement that could "deliver the best products at the best prices" without having to buy from around the world. Today, Crazy Dental Prices no longer has to bid. They work *directly* with the manufacturers to guarantee the best prices and have built systems, relationships, and volume that allow them to deliver on their lowest-price promise to buyers. They boast the lowest prices in the country for over *forty-six thousand products*.

This didn't happen only because the team at Crazy Dental Prices had a Nifty Thrifty idea. It happened because *Jay implemented ironclad systems to make it happen.* Some call his warehouse "Amazonian" with fifty people working at any given time, twenty-four hours a day, with $5–$10 million machines fulfilling orders. All automated. What started as Jay manually faxing orders has grown into a $180 million operation, and they're confident they'll hit $1 billion in the next ten years as one of the top seven distributors in the US.

Why Crazy Dental Prices' Systems Work

So how did Crazy Dental Prices do it? How did they build Crazy Dental Prices from scratch to a $180 million operation?

Not by sheer luck or chance, as Jay would attest. For him, the key was designing and implementing the best systems possible to build confidence, increase efficiency, establish consistency, and allow for scalability. Based on his story and conversations I've had with Jay, here are the key points to building those systems.

1. Build Confidence

If Jay was to build a business that relied on "gray" goods on his platform, he wouldn't feel very confident in his business or his prices. It would be a very fragile business because he'd never know if and when he wouldn't be able to continue.

He needed to do something radical: create a predictable, reliable way to guarantee the best prices without fear that his supply chain would get cut off or disrupted.

As the company built relationships with manufacturers, Jay got more confident selling. His team members also got more confident promoting it. And the customers felt confident. They know what they're getting and know they're getting it for the best prices. Moreover, Jay made sure working with Crazy Dental Prices would be a breeze for any company by providing comprehensive invoices, transferring order histories, and inputting smart customer info in their systems. Basically, working with Crazy Dental Prices was designed to be buttery smooth.

Finally, building confidence helped their manufacturers too. They know that Crazy Dental Prices has exceptional prices because of how efficient they are, not because they save money on selling "gray goods."

As a result of this confidence, anyone who worked with Jay had a more positive experience and was ready to reorder sooner, which also led to positive referrals. That's how you build confidence.

2. Increase Efficiency

There's a big reason why companies like Amazon kill it every year. When you have excellent systems in place, your company gets more efficient. Way more. You can accurately predict the time of delivery, even down to the hour. There's no need for hiring extra reps to manage orders or invoices—the system handles all of that, and in case a customer has an extra question, your team has a system to quickly take care of it.

Also, with an efficient system, say goodbye to manually invoicing your clients. Your system takes care of that too. The credit card fees are automated, and they incentivize customers to place large orders instead of small ones multiple times per week. Efficiency.

3. Establish Consistency

In this day and age, the most successful companies aren't doing most things manually. They use high-end internal software that automates everything—sales, marketing, lead gen, fulfillment, finances, you name it. This is an amazing perk of building out your systems: establishing consistency across your business. Gone are the days of each piece being managed manually and separately. If you want to grow (or just maintain) your dental practice, you need systems to create consistency and momentum across the board.

4. Document Everything

Whenever I'm thinking about creating systems for training, practice operations, or something else, I like to find a way to document it right away and then use it as a template to train the next person. That way, I don't leave anything to chance. I don't try winging it through each training session—there has to be a system to it, a method to the madness. If it works, record it and iterate on it. Improve it every time, but stick to the basics that work. That's precisely what Jay did.

Some business owners organize everything they've learned in a formal training manual. Others write out their own bullet lists and "nonnegotiables" that they impart to each recruit. My approach is to record everything I try out, then upload it all into a Google Drive. Over time, I build a database where every experience, resource, and technique is organized and ready to be used again.

From a big-picture perspective, this approach *will* save you time and money. When Jay was starting out, he didn't have dollars to spare—every cent had to count. That's probably true for you too! When you have a system in place, you don't have to invest unnecessary time and dollar bills to reinvent the wheel every time you train the next person. You have a system to fall back on. Maybe you'll get away without a system the first few times, but inevitably, you'll crave the sweet, sweet efficiency and cost savings of a system. I've seen it happen again and again.

Every Practice Has Systems

Although some practices may not have a formal manual or collection of standard operating procedure documents, don't think they don't have a system. Like you just read about in Jay's example, every practice has systems.

However, that doesn't mean every system was carefully designed, or even designed at all. Sometimes a "system" means *this is just how we do things.* Some might be inefficient. Some might be inconsistent. Despite all that, each practice has some system in place. Remember that all team members perform daily tasks based on how they were trained. Over time, this creates a system that guides how that practice runs, whether well or poorly.

Your practice works the same way. Whether your staff was all trained thoroughly on a clearly defined system, or they had no formal system to follow and had to use the "figure it out" approach, a system will emerge nonetheless.

For example, your "systems" might be inherited from former team members who left ten years ago and you have no idea why they were created in the first place. Or your system may have emerged from your team creating their own because they had none to follow.

Whatever the story, a system is inevitable, so you might as well invest time and money *now* to make sure the system works for your practice, not wait for one to pop up out of desperation.

With all that said, let me be clear: Developing a system *does not* need to be complicated or expensive. If anyone tells you that, they're either lying or selling something.

Don't waste precious resources trying to find the perfect system outside of your practice. Spoiler alert: *it doesn't exist.*

Instead, all you need is a tried-and-true blueprint to get you started, then you plug in the details. By the way, this approach can apply to any business in most industries, even if we are talking about teeth in this book.

I narrowed down this process to three simple steps and some must-haves. That's it. Like I said, don't overcomplicate it. Before you know it, your practice will level up its efficiency and production *and* make your staff feel more supported and appreciated than ever. Ready?

Identify What People Are Actually Doing in Your Practice

Ask yourself: What do you do over and over and over again? What processes repeat dozens (if not hundreds) of times every single day? Figure out what those are and list each of them. Get super detailed and leave nothing out.

After you do this, ask each staff member to do the same. I guarantee you that each team member has unique tasks they repeat each day, as well as some tasks that overlap with their teammates. This is crucial intel.

After you and your entire team have drafted your lists, review them. In no time, you'll quickly discover a few key things that are keeping you from the system of your dreams.

1. Unnecessary Tasks

You'll find tasks that are partially or downright unnecessary. Perhaps one person was trained on them, then trained the next person, then the next, and so on . . . but it's still unnecessary. Once you spot them, cut them out.

2. Inefficiencies or Redundancies

Next, you'll discover inefficiencies or redundancies. For example, you'll realize that two staff members perform the same exact task throughout the week, even though only one person needs to.

3. Assumed Tasks

Finally, you'll find tasks that you thought were being done that, at the cost of your heart health, aren't. Two team members were each assuming that the other person was handling the task, leaving the task woefully unfulfilled day after day. Not fun.

At the end of this practice, you'll have a thorough understanding of what's actually happening (and not happening) at your practice. Once you have this intel, you'll be able to start the next step of creating your very own system.

Narrow Down Your Tasks to Systematize Them

Now that you have a firm grasp of what's going on in your practice, it's time to systematize. If seeing each staff member's name makes it harder to systematize them, omit their names from the list. For now, who performs the task doesn't matter—what matters is whether your practice knows how to do it right. Just get the list in front of you so there's no confusion.

From there, organize the tasks you want to systematize by position, similar to how your job descriptions are organized. You might also find that you can update your job descriptions based on this exercise as well. Whatever you do, make sure you have a clear list of all your tasks, organized by position and priority.

Three Steps to Creating Systems That Stick

You've listed all your tasks. You've organized them by position and priority. You know what your practice needs to accomplish every single day. Now, it's time to create systems that stick. Below are three fundamental steps to get you started. Like I said in the beginning of this chapter, these three steps are just a blueprint—it's your job to fill in the details.

1. Document

This step may seem obvious, but it's the most important one. All of your tasks are listed anyway, so it's time to document them. However, don't just document them in a way that only you and certain staff would understand. Document your tasks in a way that a new team member—someone who's completely unfamiliar with your practice—could understand.

Why? Because your documentation needs to make your day to day predictable. When any team member or patient sees these steps documented, they have 100 percent confidence in what's going to happen, when it's going to happen, and how it's going to happen. Your practice doesn't exist only for dental nerds—it's for anyone who's interested in good oral hygiene (most people) and appreciates a Nifty Thrifty business (everyone).

2. Execute

Once you have the process written down and documented in an easy-to-understand fashion, hand it to one of your team members and have them execute the next task based on that process. As they move through that process, ask them to make notes about how they feel about the process.

Does it make sense from the get-go? Do they feel like they can ask for help as they complete each step? Do they get a sense of accomplishment the further they go? Don't be afraid to ask these questions and then some—you'll need all of this intel later.

3. Refine

After each team member works their way through the process, gather and record their feedback. Make necessary adjustments to refine the process. Then, do it again. And again. And one more time. Keep doing this until you're blue in the face but your process is rock solid. The most important feedback comes from the people who are doing this task day in, day out.

Here's a word of caution: Do *not* try to fit your new systems into a template that commands how your system "should" be. In my definition, there is no "should." There is just "is." So, refine until you make your system work for *your* situation, not someone else's.

Another word of caution: This isn't a one-time perfection exercise. Growth-minded practices are always finding ways to simplify, refine, and adjust their processes. Encourage your team members to recommend improvements to the systems as they implement them. This is how you'll create systems that stick.

How I Create a New Process in My Practice

Now that you have all the steps in your mind, let's put them to work. Let's go through how I would create a new process in real time.

Let's say I want to develop a new process for conducting Zoom meetings. Virtual meetings are commonplace now, so why not level up how we approach them?

The first thing I'd do is document the actual process. I would list out each step of the process:

1. Create the meeting on Zoom.
2. Fill in the meeting details and agenda.
3. Add the meeting to my calendar.
4. Invite all guests.
5. Confirm that all guests received the invitation.
6. As I'm going through the process, I'm not just writing it all down as bullet points. I'm recording it all with a screen recording software like Loom. That way, you see every single step in real time, leaving no room for confusion.

Next, I put all of this in a Google Drive folder. Then, I share it with a team member and ask them whether they understand it. If they have questions, I talk it through and adjust as necessary until they understand it.

Once the first team member understands the process, I send the file to the next team member. Rinse and repeat. Over time, this system gets more and more refined.

Here's another example: emergency exams.

When patients come in for an emergency visit, the most important issue for them is to have their concerns understood and addressed right away. That's exactly how I want them to feel as soon as they come in the door.

Patients crave a dentist who understands their issues and makes sure they'll receive quality care, no questions asked. Whatever the patient's chief complaint is, the dentist's job is to address it efficiently and effectively.

Not only should the front office who greets them know what the problem is, but the assistant should know, the doctor should know, and the treatment plan coordinator should know. Everyone involved in this emergency process should know the chief complaint, not just the patient.

To get to this point, it comes down to those crucial three steps:

1. *Document/record each step of intaking an emergency patient.*
2. *Ask each team member to execute their role in the process. If they have questions, answer them. If they don't, ask the next team member. Repeat until each team member understands it thoroughly.*

3. *Implement their feedback until the process feels rock solid across the board.*

Remember, doing all of this isn't just for your staff—it's to ensure that every patient knows what to expect and can rest easy that they'll be taken care of. That's the goal.

Here are the steps once again, boiled down to their chief function:

1. Document it.
2. Record it.
3. Execute it (live or rehearse).
4. Refine it.
5. Store it somewhere safe for easy access (e.g., Google Drive).

Bake Any Cake You Want

As you read this book, these steps are more than a recipe to bake a cake. Sure, understanding the ingredients and steps that go into something is fundamental, but becoming Nifty Thrifty really comes down to the concepts behind it all. In short, I don't want to just teach you how to bake one cake, in this case, a dental practice.

With this book, my ultimate goal is to teach you the concepts behind Nifty Thrifty so that you can, in theory, bake any cake you want. After turning the final page, you won't have to hire consultants or outside help to develop these systems for you—you can do it all yourself, which saves you time and money. Once you've developed the right mindset, you can create and adjust your systems as your practice changes.

Chapter Takeaways

- Every practice and business has its own system—either it emerges naturally, you hire a consultant for it, or you create it yourself. Creating it yourself is the Nifty Thrifty way.
- You need to thoroughly understand everything happening in your business before you systematize things.
- Follow the three crucial steps—document, execute, refine—to create systems that stick in your business. This is how you become nifty and thrifty.

Chapter 12:

Knowing Your Numbers

A few years ago, a dentist came to me in need of help. We'll call her Dr. J. When I asked her how her practice was doing, she told me it was thriving and had never been busier. Naturally, I asked, "So, what's the problem, exactly?" Then she broke it down:

Even though her practice was growing exponentially, she felt absolutely overwhelmed. She was working virtually every day, from sunrise to sunset. Her practice was a dentist's dream, yet she felt like she was living a nightmare.

She wanted me to coach her through these issues, to which I agreed. Let me tell you: her practice was a case study on how to overwork and stress yourself to the tooth. Here's what we learned:

First, I realized that Dr. J had several plans and procedures that weren't worth her time doing. Sure, they made money, but the stress they caused her and her staff wasn't worth it. Dr. J mistakenly thought that more procedures would automatically mean more success, but they only added more weight to her shoulders that she didn't need.

For example, when we looked at the numbers, she realized it wasn't worth her time to do root canals. It may have felt great to offer them, but the time cost required was simply not worth it. Instead, I encouraged Dr. J to review each procedure through a different lens: chair time and material costs.

Once Dr. J did that, she discovered that, while root canals weren't worth her time, adding more orthodontics would be a much more profitable option. Analyzing chair time and materials costs allowed Dr. J to see what procedures would actually benefit her practice long term.

For procedures like root canals that weren't worth her time, Dr. J simply referred those out, which created a win-win scenario: Dr. J fulfills procedures that make her money, and she helps other practices out by sending them referrals (which also bolsters their business relationship).

Those two numbers are important. If chair time is too much, you might need to improve your clinical skills. If material costs are too high, you might need to reevaluate materials.

What Numbers to Track

Dr. J's story reminded me how crucial it is to track your numbers, particularly chair time and material costs. If you fail to track these numbers, you'll find yourself like

Dr. J did—packing more and more into each day, wondering why you're still losing money and your sanity.

Knowing your numbers is a two-layer challenge. Let's break it down a bit further.

1. Set Your Mindset

Before you dive into the raw numbers, you need to address your mindset. You might be wondering, "Isn't there only one way to look at your numbers?" In fact, there are many ways. For example, some dentists see their numbers as reports, nothing more. Some dentists see their numbers as reflections of how well they practice dentistry or run a business, which you can imagine isn't great on someone's self-esteem. These are both wrong.

Here's what the winners see: Your numbers present a wonderful opportunity to improve your practice, profits, and personal life. They provide crucial insight and intel that allow you to see under the hood of your practice and make the necessary (if not life-changing) adjustments. Trust me, once you start seeing your numbers as opportunities, everything changes.

2. Know What to Track

The second piece of knowing your numbers is understanding what numbers you need to track, how to track them, and how to use them. You can have every single metric of your practice laid out in an Excel spreadsheet in front of you, but if you don't know how to interpret what you're seeing, you might as well be reading Egyptian hieroglyphics.

To get you started, there are three categories into which you can group your numbers. This will help you understand the what, why, and how. Plus, once you do this a few times, you'll have a template to refer to in the future. Win-win.

A. Macro

Understanding your business at a macro level will give you more clarity when you dig into the details. Think ten thousand feet or bird's eye view—an eagle needs to survey his territory before swooping down for a meal. This part is all about reviewing the big, important numbers.

This includes profit and loss, variable expenses, new patients, production, collections, and staff pay. As you firm up these numbers, you'll be able to funnel these resources into other places. For example, as you level up your understanding of your numbers, you'll better understand how to turn your bare minimum revenue today to your bare minimum profit in the future. This only happens when you know your numbers, though. If you know your bare minimum revenue that you need to make like the back of your hand, you'll become more confident, laser-focused, and creative in reaching your target numbers.

B. Micro

Micro numbers are the nitty-gritty details that some dentists (including me) love getting into. Whether you're detailed or a big-picture person, the micro details are crucial to your success.

Micro numbers include the cost of each supply, each procedure, each production by procedure, your doctor hourly production, and your hygienist hourly production, to name a few. Some of these may not feel necessary to track if your big numbers are on point, but trust me, they are. The tighter each of these numbers is, the more growth your business can handle.

C. Procedure-Specific Numbers

Procedure-specific numbers could also be called "micro micro," but that didn't sound good on paper. These are the numbers for every single procedure you offer. For example, what time and materials are needed to perform each procedure? How much time does each require? Who's performing it? Which materials and supplies are you using?

Trust me, these are the numbers that separate the good from the great practices. Don't skimp on these.

How to Get Your Numbers

At this point, you might be saying, "Glenn, how do I find these numbers? I'm not a numbers guy/gal and honestly have no idea where to look. Help!"

Don't worry, you're not alone. Living in this digital, technologically-obsessed world we live in, there are more options than ever to track down, organize, and put your numbers to good use. To help you get started, let's start with someone you *need* in your corner.

1. Partners (Bookkeepers and CPAs)

If you want to know my recommendation, it's Harsh Patel at HMP Consultants. Harsh and his team offer full-service accounting and tax solutions, and they know how to be Nifty Thrifty. They do excellent work.

Here's a wild story Harsh told me that's stuck with me for years:

Harsh was working with another business that needed some serious help. They were bleeding money even though their practice was growing, and they couldn't figure out why. As a result, they were facing a huge tax bill that they couldn't afford (a six-figure tax bill).

After Harsh and his team dove into this practice's financials and business structure, they discovered some huge mistakes that only could have happened from not reviewing their numbers.

Number one, their business structure was entirely wrong, which forced them to pay over $100,000 in unnecessary taxes to the IRS. These owners did have a CPA, but when Harsh asked why the CPA didn't tell them about the error, the practice responded, "They never got back to us about it." Talk about peace of mind!

Two, they were spending $20,000 on a marketing agency that wasn't getting them results. This agency wasn't sending reports, so the dentist had even less data to know whether they were making the right decisions.

So, to summarize, this business had both a CPA and a marketing agency that were failing to disclose numbers and data, leaving their client alone to pick up the pieces. This is the danger of not knowing your numbers.

As dire as this situation seemed, Harsh and his team knew exactly what to do and provided them with the support they *really* needed at that moment.

First, Harsh helped the practice restructure their business correctly, which saved them *literally hundreds of thousands of dollars*. As the client realized this, they told Harsh, "Oh my God, I've been throwing so much money away!"

Second, Harsh and his team connected their client with a new CPA and marketing agency, which was a major turnaround for them. Suddenly, they were getting a positive ROI for their marketing efforts, and they knew their CPA would keep their finances on track.

Additionally, when they highlighted the client's accounts receivable, they were able to begin collecting much more money, much faster.

The beauty of these two is you don't have to change anything about your practice to save money. It's all on paper, which makes it a very simple change to implement. You'd be shocked at how many "small" adjustments lead to significant changes.

Finally, Harsh helped them restructure their business to stop paying unnecessary taxes. If you're structured as an LLC and never changed it, you may be doing the same thing they were.

I find that if you haven't talked with your CPA in more than six months, you're likely being underserved and don't know your numbers well enough. Someone's not looking closely enough at your numbers to help you take action to reduce your tax burden or free up cash flow.

In the end, the greater knowledge and focus helped their client increase their bottom line, operate way more efficiently, and significantly free up precious time. It had a profound trickle-down effect across the entire practice, and it's the perfect example of what working with someone like Harsh can do for your practice. That's the power of knowing your numbers and business inside and out.

When you're searching for the right CPA for your business, there are a few crucial things you need to keep in mind:

A. Know Your Goals

First and foremost, your bookkeeper or CPA should know your goals. And I mean, *know* like they know their own practice. Every business has different goals, and you don't want your accountant to lose track of what you're trying to accomplish in the first place. Whatever your individual goals are, communicate those openly and honestly with your bookkeeper or CPA. Help them help you.

One of the next biggest ways to save money is how you expense and depreciate assets. Are you doing cost segregation studies? Are they tracking your tax returns and monthly expenses to free up cash flow? Are you taking advanced depreciation when it's available? Have you discussed with your bookkeeper or CPA how to best treat your assets to maximize your tax savings? This is especially important when you acquire a practice, or if you're building or renovating your office.

B. Have Quarterly Meetings

Having quarterly meetings isn't a given for all bookkeepers or CPAs, but it's a must for me. I'm a big believer in having quarterly meetings to evaluate our progress, as well as reassess our goals to make sure they're still aligned with our values. If your CPA doesn't offer these, I highly recommend finding another—your business needs those routine checkups.

C. Track Monthly Profit/Loss

This may sound easy to keep track of, but you'd be shocked at how quickly we lose track of this number in the flurry of running a business. However, when you hire someone whose *job* is to keep track of it, your business will thank you for it.

Not every CPA is built the same, but be patient and keep these things in mind. With time, you'll find the right one.

2. Software

If you'd rather track your numbers yourself, don't even think about tracking your numbers manually. Trust me, it won't go well. Enter practice management software.

If you've never used something like this before, these services are your one-stop shop for numbers, client data, scheduling, and more. As you input your own data (the more the better), the software will automatically keep track of your numbers in real time.

That way, reviewing your data is a breeze—just click a few buttons and voilà, you have macro numbers, micro numbers, procedure-specific numbers, and everything in between at your fingertips.

Ultimately, I still recommend hiring out. Nothing keeps you on track quite like hiring someone else to hold your feet to the fire. That's where bookkeepers and CPAs come in. As soon as you sit down in a room with smart people who understand financials and taxes, it's almost like "Poof, your tax rate is lower!" It's that miraculous, but only if you're willing to hire the right people. That's why I can't recommend Harsh and his team enough.

Use Your Numbers to Make Nifty Thrifty Decisions

Now that you know your numbers, knowing how to make Nifty Thrifty decisions is a different ball game entirely. You can lay out every single number of your practice in a meticulous way, stand in front of it . . . and have absolutely no idea what to do with the chicken scratch you're seeing. Let's change that.

Think Like Chick-fil-A

Chick-fil-A has its system down to a science, and it starts with something super simple: the classic chicken sandwich. Here's how it works:

If you were the owner of a Chick-fil-A restaurant and knew you served one hundred sandwiches this month, would you know how many pickle slices you used almost to the exact pickle, minus customization? You need that same level of awareness in your practice.

Do It Yourself

First, I want you to establish a baseline. Focus on the macro numbers that we laid out earlier—profit and loss, production, and so on. Put that number in front of you.

Next, fill in the micro details within the context of each macro. For example, what's the total cost of each procedure over the year? What's your yearly cost for all your hygienists? Add all of these up.

Also, track all of your recurring expenses and evaluate them once a year. No matter how small some of these may be, they add up by the end of the year.

After some time, you should have an outline of your year: what you need to spend, what you actually spend, and your revenue goals. Once you have these three metrics, review them monthly or quarterly with your team to make sure you're all on track.

Why are these metrics important? Because they allow you to understand exactly how profitable each procedure is, and they help you make better decisions about which insurance to accept, which procedures to perform, which procedures to promote, and so on. Knowledge is power.

Chapter Takeaways

- Understand that your numbers come down to the macro, micro, and procedure specific.
- Use partners (bookkeepers, CPAs, accountants) and/or software to keep track of your numbers.
- Think like Chick-fil-A and know your numbers inside and out in order to make Nifty Thrifty decisions with your numbers.

Chapter 13:

Spending

When I started, I could only borrow $300,000 to open my practice. So I only had $300,000 for everything, including working capital, build-out, buying equipment, etc. Of that $300,000, the bank only allowed me to use $70,000 for working capital because they wanted the other money to be used to purchase equipment and other assets they could take back if I failed to pay. As you might imagine, it taught me some valuable lessons that I take with me to this day.

One lesson I quickly learned was how you don't need millions of dollars to start a practice that attracts patients—*you just need to spend what you do have on what matters and get results from it.* I believe this approach helped me grow my business (and more importantly my mindset) far faster than any check would have.

For example, I spent as little money as possible on the original carpeting and lighting in my office, but I invested three or four times as much for the carpeting and lighting in the waiting and patient rooms. The bathroom the staff and I used was very basic, but I spent far more on decorating the patients' bathroom. My philosophy was, if my patients can see it, I need to invest in it. Why? Because that carpeting, lighting, and waiting room were my marketing.

Remember the marketing and networking I described earlier? I couldn't afford any of that extra stuff, but I knew that if I made a stellar impression on the patients I did have, they would be more likely to come back and refer me. In a way, that was my marketing and networking. It was all word-of-mouth, and I had made the absolute best of it.

At the same time, I was very mindful of the fixed costs involved that I couldn't reduce, namely rent and utilities. However, if I noticed space on the second floor of a building with great visibility, I knew that kind of visibility could serve my practice well for decades. Like I said, it was about spending money on the things that mattered—things that attracted patients and served them well for years to come. With time, the money would come.

When I expanded, I bought used chairs but changed the upholstery. I have ten operatories right now, but only two of those I purchased new—the others I bought used and refinished them. My goal is to find equipment that will last a lifetime, which makes the investment worthwhile.

Did I get the best of the best of everything? No, but I did wherever patients could see it. That's what mattered. I wanted to make sure that everything my patients saw was high-end and high class.

For my team, I spare no expense in making sure they get the best training. When they hit their goals, I reward them well.

Even today, there's only so much money, no matter how much you're making.

While most people think about supplies when it comes to spending, it's important to remember that when you invest in people you get the best ROI. The reason being is they ultimately help you produce more and grow your practice more.

When it comes to Nifty Thrifty spending, I want you to focus on four major categories: supplies, vendors, team, and infrastructure.

Above all, don't fret about how much you "should" make. That's irrelevant right now. All that matters is how to utilize what you do have and cherish every penny. Trust me, that mindset will get you much further than you having all the money in the world without a lick of sense on how to use it.

Spending on Supplies

When it comes to spending on supplies, the one thing you have to remember is that prices fluctuate. That's a given truth of the market and running your own business. If you're looking for less risk, you might be in the wrong trade. But if you can handle it, the secret is those who pay the most attention will save the most money. Don't fear price fluctuations—just roll with them and know when to strike.

For every business owner I work with, I ask them this question: "Why do you want to save money?"

Does that sound like a strange question? Believe it or not, it isn't. I ask because I want to see where the owner's heart is. Saving money isn't inherently a good thing if your goal is to line your pockets while your practice suffers.

My philosophy is that being smart with money enables you to invest in your people and patients, which (I believe) inevitably makes you money. If you do this right, you can create a prosperous cycle of saving and investing in your practice.

Spending on Vendors

Shop Around

How much do you spend on phones every month? On Wi-Fi? Do you know? If you don't, you're not alone. Most businesses I work with don't either, and that's a problem.

When you shop for one of these services, it's easy to assume that the first number you hear is the *only* offer available. But in reality, don't judge a book by its cover. For example, if you get a price point from Option A, go to Option B and ask whether they can match that. If not, try Option C. If Option C can match or even beat Option

A's offer, then you've just saved money, my friend. Don't be afraid to shop around.

Know Your Contracts

Secondly, it's crucial that you understand your contracts. Can you find out exactly what you're spending on vendors within five minutes? If you can't, I was you once. However, I soon learned that it's not enough to just remember how much you spend monthly or yearly—you need to know exactly what you're contractually obligated to.

In my case, I organize all of my contracts in a free Google spreadsheet or binder. Within five minutes, I can tell you exactly what I'm spending. That's powerful.

Find the Right Partners

Finally, if you pay someone to do your marketing, listen closely. Remember the practice that was spending $20,000 a year on a marketing agency that wasn't getting them results? Even though they do the grunt work, it's your responsibility to partner with them to ensure that leads are coming in, where they're coming from, and how much they're costing you. If they won't or can't, you need to find a vendor who will.

Having the right partners as vendors is key. They need to be able to get you the information you need to understand whether you're spending money wisely and to be able to make smarter decisions with your money. Don't leave anything here to chance.

Spending on Your Team

As I said earlier, I don't hold anything back when compensating my team. If they do excellent work, they've earned their pay. Simple. That's why we have a pay grade system: you pay your team based on the skills they bring to the practice.

Controlled Spending

We don't believe in giving people raises just because they've stayed with us for a certain period of time—an "existence tax." We pay them based on the value they provide to the practice. Why? Because this approach keeps spending under control. Controlled spending doesn't mean that you're going to lay off people or shortchange them. Controlled spending means that they're continuously earning their paycheck or providing more value to the practice than what you pay them so you can continue to operate profitably. Align your team's pay with their ability to bring in more money, and everybody grows together.

Paying for Training

Continually train your team members and add incentives for them to train their subordinates. Remember, someday your rock stars will leave, and if you don't have someone to replace them, you're going to take a hit. Don't forget, you're a member of the team as well, so you need to make sure you're spending wisely on helping yourself level up.

If there's one thing I want you to remember when it comes to CE and other training, it's this: your ROI doesn't come from the education but from the execution.

Hiring for Growth

When you're looking to hire, hire for growth. We believe in hiring for mindset over skill set. That may sound absurd, but here's why we do it: It's easy to train a new recruit in the skills they need, but their mindset must be ingrained. Even if an applicant has all of the necessary skills, if they don't align with your practice's values, those skills won't matter when they're creating conflict.

Here's another reason: If you hire someone who's extremely experienced, they have little to no room to grow in your practice. They'll get you results, but they'll also leave for higher pay before you know it, which will cost you more in the long run. Instead, hire someone who can learn quickly and grow in your practice—that hire will yield a much better ROI over the long run.

Another thing: We all know what it's like to hire a bad employee. But you know what? Most of the time, an employee is "bad" because they don't align with the practice's values, not because they don't have the necessary skills. You can teach those skills, but you can't teach a better attitude. Trust me, *I've tried*. The more you try to force a square peg into a round hole, the more you damage your practice's culture.

So, the secret to becoming a successful entrepreneur in any industry is *execution*. Everyone has a good idea. Everyone can learn new skills. What separates the successful people from the others is execution. The successful people actually get things done and put the square pegs in the square holes.

It might sound like I'm repeating myself, and that's because I am. I want to hammer these points into your head to make sure you process the information and *actually apply it.* That's how you Nifty Thrifty.

Spending on Infrastructure

Infrastructure and equipment is one of those categories that strikes fear into the hearts of any dentist and business owner. "How will I know whether I'm getting my money's worth? What happens if something doesn't work or breaks? Should I always buy new, or will the refurbished one work?" These are valid questions that, trust me, I struggled with when I was starting out.

Imagine you've just opened your practice and are ready to bring in the equipment. The first thing you need to ask yourself is whether it's a need or a want. For example, if you want a new intraoral scanner, I understand. It's cool. But before you pull the trigger, ask yourself whether it's truly a need or just a want. Are you going to use it enough right away to justify the investment? Or can it wait a little until you get your patient volume up to the point it justifies making the purchase?

If you're considering expanding, is it a luxury or is the demand there for it? Are your patients waiting three months or more to get an appointment, and that piece of equipment will fulfill that need? Or is it something that *might* be used once in a while, but it'll otherwise sit in a corner collecting dust?

If you want to renovate, are people complaining about the current state of your practice? Are people saying things about your practice in reviews? Are you attracting the wrong patients?

Because infrastructure spending can be big and involve debt, it's critically important to evaluate the costs carefully and understand whether they're a need or a want. This will help you avoid unnecessary purchases and stick to what your practice needs.

Nifty Thrifty Spending

No matter what you're spending your money on, the key to making it Nifty Thrifty is this: It's not about paying less on everything; it's about smart spending and spending on what matters. It's about tracking all of your important numbers and making conscious decisions on them every single day.

I didn't get to where I am because I had infinite money—far from it. Any successful dentist and business owner will echo what I'm about to say: Success comes from doing the best with what you have and getting results from it. That's it. That's the key to Nifty Thrifty spending. You'll already have plenty to spend money on (payroll, rent, etc.), so take advantage of free software, shop around for your vendors, and don't be afraid to know every detail of your contracts. Being Nifty Thrifty isn't a one-and-done transaction—it's a choice you make every day. Make your spending decisions like that.

Chapter Takeaways

- Know your four spending categories: supplies, vendors, your team, and infrastructure.
- Don't be afraid to shop around and meticulously track your spending—your business demands it.
- Nifty Thrifting spending is about getting results with the best you can afford, cherishing every penny along the way.

Chapter 14:

Negotiating Win-Wins

The owner of one of the best burger places in town is a patient of mine, and I love him. More times than I could count, I used to eat at his restaurant and strike up a conversation every time we ran into each other. We'd fill each other in on our lives, how our families and businesses were doing, normal guy stuff.

At one point, I remember telling him about how my practice offers benefits to all of our team, and I naturally asked whether he did the same with his employees. He admitted he did not. At that moment, I didn't judge him or think I was better—I saw it as an incredible opportunity. I offered to extend my discount plan to him and anyone on his team who became a patient with us.

As a result, I got many new patients there, he and his team got dental insurance, and I'm now known as *his* dentist, not just *a* dentist. This means that whenever someone asks him where to find a good dentist, if I do my job right, he'll respond with "You can check out *my* dentist." See? That's the power of creating win-wins.

The beautiful part of this system is that, if you can imagine it, you can probably create a win-win scenario for it. Think about all the small business owners in your community. Think about anyone who has extended family or a team who might not have insurance. Think of the police chief, the government official, or the used car dealership. If you can imagine it, there's probably a win-win scenario out there.

Something I should point out: In the restaurant industry, it's rare for business owners to be able to offer dental insurance to their team members. It just doesn't happen most of the time. Knowing this, I offered him a free discount plan membership for himself plus a discounted membership plan for his team members if he referred people to my practice and helped promote me. That's what we call a "win-win."

The Master of Win-Wins, Sean Ryan

One exemplar of negotiating win-wins is my friend Sean Ryan. He runs the online service division for Medidenta, an independent dental supply company that helps dental practices make smarter and more informed (Nifty Thrifty) decisions in their practice. In addition to the amazing win-wins he's doing over there, Sean also helps folks in the Nifty Thrifty community save tons of money in their own practices in ways that benefit them, their suppliers, and their patients. In short, win-wins for everyone.

In my opinion, Sean is a master at the art of negotiating win-wins. Over the years I've known him, I've seen him demonstrate his mastery through a step-by-step process that, every time he does it, helps everyone. Here's what I've learned:

1. Assess Your Present Circumstances

Before you try to get win-wins in your practice, it's imperative that you understand where your practice is right now. Basically, when it comes to negotiation, what's your practice's default? Do you lean toward getting wins for your patients or your practice? Once you understand where your practice is, you'll be better equipped to make the switch to a win-win structure.

For example, many dental practices order their supplies through catalogs and salespeople. That's the status quo for practices because it's easy. They don't have to do a lot of work to find what they're looking for. Flip through some pages, pick what you want, and click order or call the phone number. Easy, but it's rarely the best option.

Most suppliers offer all of their products in a thick catalog, some of which had over nine hundred pages. Each page is colorful and enticing, begging you to turn the page to see what dental gadget you can add to your office. The strategy is simple: sell as much as possible, whether or not the practice *actually* needs it.

Sean saw this as anything but win-win. The strategy tilts the advantage in the dental supply company's favor and away from the practice. The more they sell, regardless of whether the practice needs it, the better off they are. Plus, these companies would send out their best salespeople (with snacks and other "incentives") to persuade you to pull the trigger. Win for the supply company. Lose for the dental practice.

Once he understood that this is where most dental practices started, he knew how and why he needed to flip the script. By implementing the right strategy, he could change the narrative from win-lose to win-win.

2. Know What and Why You're Negotiating

As Sean set out to create win-wins in the dental supply space, he and Medidenta decided to take a radical approach: *sell direct*. That's right, Sean doesn't sell anything through a colorful, nine-hundred-page catalog, coupled with persuasive salespeople. Not one. Everything they sell is direct, working closely with each practice to negotiate those win-wins.

To make this approach profitable, however, Sean quickly realized he had some work ahead of him. First off, he had a lot of homework to do—he had to be 100 percent sure that his win-win *in theory* was win-win *in practice for every unique practice*. Second, Sean realized that a demanding approach *was poison to negotiation*. No one wants to feel strong-armed into an agreement. Instead, Sean focused on talking every deal through and arriving at something that felt so win-win that both parties knew right away.

Finally, Sean discovered that too many practices fixate on the *brand* rather than the *quality* of a product, which makes dental practices think they have limited quality options. Sean changed this narrative by focusing on the *quality of the product or service*.

For example, if a dental practice is in the market for a Prophy Magic angle, Sean knows how to match that dental practice with a similar product with identical quality *for half the price*. Sean firmly believes that, with a little homework and the right partners, dental practices can easily find those win-wins. That's the power of focusing on quality, not just brand.

Here are some more key pointers I've learned from Sean: When you're shopping for products across different suppliers, make sure you're comparing apples to apples. A huge mistake dentists make is comparing two incomparable products or supplies because price is the only factor they're focusing on. *Don't let the price dominate the conversation*, or you'll have practices settling for less due to budget and suppliers vying for a higher price tag. Make sure it's always apples to apples.

Also, do your research! I can't tell you how many times I've talked to dentists who didn't get a fair shake because they didn't adequately understand *everything* they're getting, exactly how much it'll cost, and how to make it a win-win. We're dealing with people's livelihoods here, so these are not transactions we can take lightly.

3. Broker a Deal You're Psyched to Talk About

One Saturday night, Sean offered a code to a dental practice that would help them save money when they ordered some supplies they needed. All of a sudden, unbeknownst to Sean, that dental practice shared that code with other dentists, which got Sean and Medidenta *three* more orders.

This situation was awesome for a few reasons. Not only did it save several dentists money, but it also *created a community between all of those dentists and Sean.* Instead of each practice going through a catalog, unaware they could find a better deal elsewhere, Sean helped Medidenta, the original dentist, and many more practices save money *and get to know others in their field.*

That's what happens when you broker deals you're excited about: *They have the power to transform multiple practices on multiple levels.* That's why Sean loves doing it: the idea of sharing a coupon that helps multiple parties save a lot of money (sometimes upward of 20 percent), creates a community between them, *and* generates more clientele for Medidenta—that's a deal anyone would get excited about. That's the power of win-win.

How to Negotiate Win-Wins in Your Practice

Back in the day, before social media and running water, the way you networked with people was by going to meetings. You went to the Chamber of Commerce meetings. You showed up to Rotary Club meetings. You attended whatever local networking event was happening in your town. You couldn't just hit "Connect" or "Add Friend" on your computer screen to meet someone—you had to put yourself out there to get known.

Nowadays, so many business owners default to the easy button, clicking and instant messaging. People all want to go online, and I understand why. Social media networking has its place.

But the tried-and-true method is still in-person, no matter what decade you're living in.

If you're newer at in-person networking or don't know how to maximize your results, don't worry. Just like everything in this book, there's a method to the madness. Here are four steps to help you put yourself out there and grow like you know you should.

1. Understand Your Goal

Before you drive over to that networking event, business cards in hand, you need to know *exactly* why you're going. It's not enough to say, "Meet people and get more business." That's too vague.

For example, you could be going to find more suitable vendors to help you save money on supplies and infrastructure. Or, perhaps you're going to meet new potential patients, particularly ones who haven't had the best experience with dentists in the past. Whatever it is, define your goal and walk in those doors with the confidence that you know why you're there.

2. Identify the Key People Involved

The next step is to identify the key people involved in this hypothetical win-win. For example, you could be trying to negotiate a win-win for your vendors, team members, or patients. Make sure you're precise about who's involved in this discussion, as it'll help you strive for their best interests in your negotiation.

3. Learn What They Want

After you identify who's involved, your responsibility is now to understand what that party wants. So, if you're trying to negotiate a win-win with your vendors and your practice, it's crucial that you understand what's in it for your vendors. What are their dreams, desires, needs, fears, and so on? You may have a general idea of their needs, but don't assume—do your research and, if you can, *just ask*. Never underestimate the power of simply asking the right questions.

4. Create a Win-Win Structure

Okay, so you've understood your goal, identified the key people involved, and learned what the party(s) involved wants. Now, it's time to put that knowledge to work. It's time to create a win-win structure, just like the one I created with that restaurant owner.

Before you read about this process applied in real time, I want you to remember one thing: Don't worry about following every step verbatim. Don't fret if your process looks slightly (or even drastically) different from my example. Although the fundamentals of business ownership are the same, every business has unique needs and audiences. These examples are meant to serve as a blueprint, just like everything in this book.

Below are some of my favorite examples that showcase the win-win structure at work.

Win-Wins with Your Team

Whenever I think about win-wins in my own practice, I think across the board. Meaning, I don't focus only on creating an isolated case that rarely happens again. I dedicate myself to designing our entire practice around the idea of win-win.

This is especially important as it relates to my team. I want to design win-win systems and processes that are baked into every thread of our practice. Every day they come into work, they automatically know that when I win, they win, no matter what.

The key to doing this is understanding your team's hopes and dreams. They obviously want to work in dentistry, but what else? What do they dream and worry about during and outside of work?

For example, if one of my team members writes books in their spare time and wants more time to do so, I would tailor their position to where if they hit certain milestones, they get additional time off or can work remotely.

Or let's say one of my hygienists loves DJ Smiles and would be head over heels to meet him. If she knocked out her workload and delivered results, I would take her to an event where John is speaking. She would get the opportunity to learn from one of the best and feel treated, and our entire practice would move the needle forward. Win-win.

Win-Wins in Your Community

Nothing says "I'm invested in our community's growth and success" like a win-win. The burger shop example is a classic case of win-win, but that's not the only one you can do. Sean demonstrates this through the power of referral: If a dental practice is negotiating with him and Medidenta, Sean will offer to introduce that practice to his colleagues. The goal? Find an even better deal now that more people are involved. Now, more people are connected *and* just secured a killer deal because of it.

I can't tell you the number of times I've said some version of "If you have family or friends who don't have dental insurance, I'd be happy to help them at the same discounted rate." It's so simple, but its efficacy rate is outrageous. Why? Because people want clean teeth and love feeling taken care of.

Also, you have a tremendous opportunity to build trust and rapport with your colleagues. For example, one of the biggest tactics Sean imposed on me is to *be transparent with price changes*. For most suppliers, they'll just hike the price up, not tell you, and expect you to carry on business as usual . . . *which often works*.

However, Sean believes you can create massive win-wins in your community through price increases. How? Because you have an opportunity to offer a partnership where they'll save money and join an awesome community. For example, if a practice becomes a Nifty Thrifty member, it'll pay the same price over the next ten years and *not have to worry about unexpected price hikes*. That's a huge opportunity to create a win for them (no price hikes!) and a win for me (more members to help improve their practices). Win-win.

Win-Wins with Your Vendors

Remember when I told you not to take a vendor's offer at face value? To shop around and find the best deal for your practice? You can apply the same tactic to create win-wins with those vendors.

How do you do this? First off, you start with what they want. By and large, vendors crave security in their clientele. They want to know that they'll keep clients for a predictable period of time, avoiding churn (another word for turnover) as much as possible.

I can use this wisdom to both of our advantage. For example, let's say I want to create a win-win with my practice's Wi-Fi vendor. Internet service providers (ISPs) want to retain monthly clients and avoid churn just like everybody else, so I already know what they want.

Here's what I'd tell them: If I can get a certain range of prices from you for a specified period of time (typically six months to one year), then I'll sign up right now. If not, I'll look elsewhere. If they say yes, I send them a spreadsheet of exactly what I need for how long I need it. I'm crystal clear. As long as you treat me well and stick to the price we agreed to, you've got a consistent client on your roster. Win-win.

The "Take the Pressure Off" Philosophy

All of this win-win comes back to the idea of taking the pressure off someone. In the burger shop example, notice that I didn't apply the pressure by asking him, "Hey, who's your dentist?" It may sound like an innocent question, but in reality, he would have felt awkward immediately. Whether or not he would have told me, I guarantee he would have felt like I was trying to pressure him into a deal. That is *not* Nifty Thrifty.

Remember what I asked instead: "Do you offer benefits to your team?" Suddenly, he didn't feel pressured because he knows I'm not some insurance broker. However, it created an amazing opportunity to hook him and his team up with benefits they need. In essence, I didn't pressure him to buy what I'm selling, which would be a win-lose scenario. I highlighted a need in his life, gave him a spectacular deal on how to fulfill the need, and demonstrated how it would help both of us. Win-win.

Using "No-Negotiation" Win-Wins I've Negotiated for You

If you've read all of this and are still thinking, "Glenn, this all makes sense, but I need concrete examples. I need to see win-wins already done," I've got you covered. In the world of Nifty Thrifty, I've already negotiated plenty of win-win deals for you at NiftyThriftyDentists.com.

This isn't just a website for dentists, although we can speak your language if you are. This website is for showcasing the power of Nifty Thrifty, illustrating what happens when you create Nifty Thrifty deals across your business, industry, and community.

If you love what you see and want to jump into the action, I've got two steps for you: First, search through the catalog of deals at NiftyThriftyDentists.com. Then, become part of our community in our very own Facebook group, Nifty Thrifty Dentists.

Chapter Takeaways

- Think of the burger shop example: the art of win-win is about being in the right place at the right time, asking the right questions.
- Negotiating win-wins happens in three key places: your team, your community, and your vendors.
- Take the pressure off people and stop trying to gain business through win-lose arrangements—focus on win-win every time.

Chapter 15:

Growth

When Jeff Guidie was building 4G Dental Lab, his focus was always on the sale transaction. His mantra was this: Whenever you're headed somewhere that could be a sales pitch, assume it is. Prepare your materials and be ready to pitch. For Jeff, that's how he grew 4G Dental Lab to the behemoth it is today. But let me be clear: It wasn't about selling the cheapest product to get someone to say yes. Instead, Jeff's philosophy was all about growing in two key areas: how 4G was different, and how 4G was better.

This relates to something people so often miss about growth. Whether you're starting or growing a business, there's an umbrella over everything you do. How you train and compensate your employees impacts your products, which impacts your patients, and so forth. Everything in your business is underneath this umbrella. So, Jeff leveraged that to grow 4G—every decision they made had to point toward being better than other labs out there.

Here's another growth hack I learned from Jeff: Nobody can say "No." If someone is uncomfortable with a customer request, it automatically rolls up to Jeff, who can make the final decisions based on what's best for 4G. Otherwise, they can confidently say "Yes" to customers and know they're not going to get in trouble. I love this approach to growth because it eliminates the bottleneck of having to go to Jeff for *every* decision that's even slightly out of the ordinary course of business and builds trust between Jeff and his team. They know Jeff has their back on their "Yes" decisions and is available to help make decisions they're uncomfortable making themselves.

Why Jeff is Nifty Thrifty

There are hundreds of other dental labs out there, but Jeff didn't care about that. His focus was simple: be different and be better at it. To do this, he designed 4G on four foundational principles: God, Grateful, Goodness, and Green, hence the appropriate name. From there, every decision was made through the filter of those four principles. Every employee, partner, and patient knew about them too. Jeff was ultra intentional about these four, which helped him grow with the right people. Plus, embedding these principles cultivates deeper relationships with everyone involved. Patients trust you, employees feel valued, and partners come to you.

This is so similar to how I approach the Nifty Thrifty community. We have literally hundreds of thousands of people in our community, yet I keep getting messages about how supported everyone feels. This didn't happen by accident, trust me. We created an ecosystem of support and resources that dentists could turn to. Our community gives a voice to dentists and those in the dental community. People partner with us, including Jeff and 4G Dental Lab, because they feel close to us due to our leadership and positive influence. That's how we built Nifty Thrifty Dentists, and it's how Jeff built 4G Dental Lab with his clientele. In Jeff's words, "Give them that good ol' Southern hospitality!"

Choose Your Own Adventure

Before we jump into this final chapter, I have one important question to ask you: *How do you want to grow?* Take some time to think about it before reading on. I want you to be as transparent and detailed with yourself as you can.

We've covered how to adopt an owner mindset, foster leadership in your business, develop skills in you and your team, cultivate personal growth, shift from the operatory to the boardroom, create a team mindset, recruit, compensate your team, train your team, retain your people, develop rock-solid systems, know your numbers, spend money on what matters, and negotiate win-wins across your practice. Now, it's time to *actually grow this thing you're building.*

Do you want to grow your personal life? Do you crave work-life balance? Or would you rather grow like a dental Monopoly Man? Whatever your path may be, your growth path will depend on your primary goal. Most importantly, remember that there's no right answer here—it all depends on where you feel called to go.

If you implement everything we've discussed in this book, one step at a time, you'll be shocked at how well your practice begins to operate. You'll uncover new ways to practice dentistry and make a difference in your patients' lives. It's almost like I designed it that way.

Begin with the End in Mind

Before you start striving for your dream outcome, you have to begin with the end in mind. For example, do you want to be more present at home and not work as much? Or do you love the idea of becoming the next dental tycoon whose life centers around their practice?

Whatever your goal is, it's your responsibility to define it and map the steps you need to take to get there. More-over, you need to define *why* your goal is important to you. Being the next dental tycoon isn't inherently better than craving a work-life balance—it's your life, so you decide why it's important.

In my experience, I believe there are three primary paths you can take, each demanding more of your time and attention. Let's review them.

Three Types of Dentists to Grow Into

1. Lifestyle Dentist

This path is for those who prefer an easier, more relaxed approach in their career. If you're a lifestyle dentist, you enjoy being a dentist, but you don't want it to interfere with your personal life. You prefer a low-stress work environment. You crave a well-balanced lifestyle. In short, you don't want to spend most of your waking hours in the office. You work to live, not live to work.

This path is excellent for those who prioritize their family and want to maximize time with them. You love what you do, but it isn't your life. As you can imagine, this path is the least aggressive and the most gradual. Growth will be slow but steady, allowing you to invest your time where it matters.

2. Entrepreneur Dentist

In terms of time and energy investment, this is the next step up. Being an entrepreneur dentist is all about maximizing revenue while minimizing time needed from you. This frees up as much time for yourself as you want without sacrificing income. In my opinion, this is the holy grail of dentistry.

You get to make as much money as you want while keeping your operations relatively contained and simple. Your stress is relatively close to that of a lifestyle dentist, but your potential for growth and revenue is substantially higher. At this point, you're likely making a great living and enjoying your life.

To transition from a lifestyle dentist to an entrepreneurial one, you'll likely have to add high-value procedures to make a similar income while keeping your time investment in check. As you grow, you'll need to establish your long-term goals and make sure you spend time and money where it really matters.

3. Tycoon Dentist

If you're itching to go even further and don't mind the time and energy investment, this option is for you. If you're a lifestyle or entrepreneur dentist and want to become a tycoon, the roads split from here. You'll have to make a sizable resource investment to get here.

Being a tycoon dentist looks like scaling to two or more locations, slowly building an empire. This option isn't for those who care about work-life balance. Being a tycoon dentist gives you the freedom to grow as far and wide as you desire.

A word of caution if you're considering this path: If you want to grow to multiple locations, you need to add new procedures to your repertoire. If you simply try to add a location on top of everything you are currently doing in the one location, you'll burn out. Instead, identify the right people to help you in your current practice so you can split your attention as you expand. That's the key to becoming a tycoon dentist.

No matter what path you choose, the solution is a combination of skills and people. What skills do you need to succeed in your desired direction? What kind of people do you need around you to lead and support you in that direction? Let's expand on the skill sets and people in these three types of dental paths.

Skills Needed to Grow in Each Path

1. Lean and Mean Lifestyle

Since your primary focus is on your personal life, not your professional career, staying on top of your clinical work is a must. You need to be ahead of the game, every single day, to maintain the engine of your practice vehicle.

Next, your responsibility is to build a team and systems that can attract the right number and quality of patients to fuel the engine. You'll rely more on outsourcing to the right vendors than building internal teams like you might do as an entrepreneur or tycoon dentist.

Finally, you'll want to keep things very simple and not hire too many people or associates. Your priority is your lifestyle, so your practice needs to stay lean and mean in order to keep your life mostly stress-free.

2. Efficient and Delegating Entrepreneur

Your focus is now on maximizing revenue while minimizing time needed from you, so you'll need different skills if you don't want to be chairside all day. You're the hardest worker in the room, but your goal isn't to show off. Instead, you'll be more of a mentor, motivating your associates and staff to produce like you.

Also, you'll need to be good at delegating tasks. Delegating is one of the key determining factors between mediocre and great entrepreneurs, so if you want to maximize production without sinking hundreds of hours into something, this is a must.

You might also want to start hiring more internal help for marketing as the volume increases. Like I just mentioned, a successful entrepreneur delegates tasks to someone who can do it better and more efficiently, saving time and money.

Finally, similar to the lifestyle dentist, you'll want to keep your operations relatively simple and contained. This is how you'll make as much money as possible without sacrificing your lifestyle. That's the key to being an entrepreneur dentist.

3. C-Suite and Corporate Tycoon

If you're looking to become a tycoon, you can't think like a dentist anymore. Now, you have to think like a C-Suite executive, looking to build an empire of multiple locations and systems that grow for a lifetime, however big you want.

To do this, you need to recruit and lead other C-level people to run parts of your growing practice portfolio. These star players are instrumental in growing your empire and running everything well. A CEO is only as good as the weakest person around them, so make sure you find the best ones. You'll build more internal teams for marketing, HR, and other services that you previously outsourced.

Furthermore, if you desire to grow big, you'll also need to learn and do well with raising funds for future expansion and growth. Every CEO knows how important it is to learn how to ask for funding, and if you're serious about being a tycoon, you will too. Finally, you'll realize you can't oversee every practice on your own and have to hire it out. This is where corporate team members come in, who will act like district managers for different locations.

What Resources Do You Need?

With all of that said, you're probably wondering, "So Glenn, what do I need to grow in each of these paths? Do I need to go to extra Rotary meetings?"

That may help, but in reality, the two main resources you'll need are *time* and *money*. That's it. That's all anybody has in this life and in this business. With each level, you'll need to invest more time and money to make it happen. For the lean and mean lifestyle dentist, you'll need the least. But to become a tycoon dentist, you'll need far more.

Time

For example, how much time do you have to spare? As a lifestyle dentist, that spare time will be put into your lifestyle. No problem. Your practice is efficient and low-stress enough. But if you're an entrepreneur or tycoon, you'll need to free up time and invest it in delegating those tasks to your associates and internal team. Your time must be used more and more strategically as you grow.

Money

Second, do you have money to invest in training, more space, equipment, etc.?

Remember, we are all about being smart with our resources. It's about being Nifty Thrifty in everything, right? But if your vision requires other resources, the money has to come from somewhere. And the more you transition from lifestyle to entrepreneur and beyond, the more capital you'll need to make it happen. When you level up, your team has to level up too.

You'll need more equipment. Different equipment. Different relationships with labs and other vendors. Probably more space, whether only for your practice or for ones you expand into. If you want to scale your dental practice, you also have to scale your team.

Taking a start-up to $1 million requires a certain set of skills. Taking it to $2 million takes another. So on and so forth. As you grow to a multimillion-dollar practice, you will need to add people and get completely out of the clinical work and into the boardroom.

That all takes money. If you don't build your systems around producing more of it as efficiently as possible, you'll quickly find yourself stuck as you try to scale and expand. Trust me, it's not fun to get stuck halfway up the mountain.

It all comes down to the same idea I've been hammering into your brain: be strategic with investing in resources that lead you where you want to go, whether you want to be a lifestyle, entrepreneur, or tycoon dentist.

Things to Consider as You Grow

Don't forget about asset protection. As you grow, the target on your back also grows. You should always invest in protecting your assets, but that only becomes more apparent as you move up the ladder.

Another thing: Do you only want to grow your single practice, or do you crave a second or third? And if you do grow into multiple practices, how much will each of them grow? What will they demand to continue their growth?

Finally, remember that no path is better than another. Your path is different from mine, so you may resonate with one of these growth paths way more than I do. That's okay. That's great, actually. It means that the industry of dentistry is alive and well. Let's celebrate that and grow together, shall we?

Chapter Takeaways

- There are three paths to growth in dentistry: lifestyle dentist, entrepreneur dentist, and tycoon dentist.
- Each path of growth requires certain skills to meet the new responsibilities and grow consistently.
- Each path also demands different time and money investments, with both resources becoming more precious as you move up the ladder.

Conclusion and Invitation

I t is at this point in many "how-to" books where the author invites you to join a high-ticket implementation program. And although many of those are very effective, my goal with this book has been to prepare you to implement so you don't need me. I won't abandon you, of course. You can always connect with me in the free Nifty Thrifty Dentists Facebook group, which I highly recommend.

However, I do want to share with you one of the most important messages my pastor shared with me in church one Sunday morning because that message has helped me immensely in all areas of my life, and I believe it could help you too.

The main takeaway from his sermon was that when things aren't going our way, it's perfectly natural to feel frustrated, stressed, incompetent, or like you have no control over the future.

So what do most people do when they feel like things aren't going their way? Nothing. Most just feel frustrated and accept that "their reality" is different from others. But what about those who want to do something? What do they do? In the church world, many people are encouraged to "pray harder" for God to provide. In the secular world, many are encouraged to "work harder." And, of course, in some circles, people are told to do both, pray harder and work harder.

As a person of faith, I'll never suggest that God can't singlehandedly change the direction of our future. I believe God truly can do that, and more. But what my pastor suggested we do is not to just "pray harder," as if all of our results come from God's efforts and there's nothing we can do to impact our future. He encouraged us to both pray harder *and* work harder, to pray as if everything relies on God but work as if everything relies on us. Why? Because that's where the magic happens.

The way I see it, our results come when we do both, and this is what my pastor encouraged me to do. When things are tough, or when we have goals for a bigger, better, more fulfilling future, the best next steps are almost always to lean into a higher power—in my case to God—while at the same time working harder and smarter. Why? Because God, or whatever higher power you tap into, rarely delivers results directly. Instead, God often responds to prayer with opportunities. If we pray for a more productive team, God rarely makes our current team members immediately more productive. Instead, God reveals systems to you that you can implement to increase productivity or fills a team member search with candidates who work hard and contribute to a positive culture.

You might not feel *completely* out of control in your practice. Maybe you only feel a little discomfort, like things could use optimizing, or you want to earn a little more money or free up an additional day from clinical care.

Whatever your situation, I encourage you to both pray hard and work hard. If you're a person of faith, that might mean literally praying to God for opportunities and direction. If you're not, it might mean just looking for opportunities that seem to arise out of nowhere as you work hard. I'm confident you'll find opportunities to lead you forward that you would never have seen if you were not working hard and looking for opportunities like this.

The truth is, there's so much about your results that you cannot control. But that's okay. One thing you *can* control is yourself. So when you're faced with obstacles or a circumstance you want to overcome, consider that a call to action to work hard and look for opportunities that arise as you work. If you're a person of faith, that might include praying to God. If not, it might look slightly different. But the result is the same: seeing the opportunities that seemingly fall in front of you when you're loyal and consistent in your work.

As you do, I'm confident it is only a matter of time before you find the peace, profits, and freedom you desire. As the famous speaker, author, and pastor Robert Schuller famously said, "Tough times don't last, tough people do."

Having made it through this book, I know you're tough. I know you want more. I know you're committed.

The only question is whether you continue to work hard, pray hard, and keep going.

If you do, I know there's nothing you can't achieve. I use this mindset in everything I do, from writing a book to investing in businesses to growing and improving my dental practice.

As you do, stay connected with me. Join the Nifty Thrifty Dentists Facebook group. Contact me through NiftyThriftyDentists.com. Reach out to me whenever you need direction or a connection. Reach out to me directly for anything that comes to mind, small or large, when it comes to improving your practice. I'm here to help.

I know you can do it. And I'm honored to be able to help.

Afterword by Duane Tinker, CEO of Dental Compliance Specialists

When I got into the business of helping dentists and dental practices navigate the complex landscape of dental compliance in 2011, I did so with a singular goal of helping "the little guy" avoid big problems.

My heart had always felt pulled toward solo practitioners, and that's what I did for years. Before opening my business, I worked in law enforcement for the state of Texas for ten years. I also worked as an emergency medical technician for twenty years, which gave me a front-row seat to all kinds of medical situations. Together, those experiences gave me many great years and opportunities to lay the foundation for how I now help dentists and practices through Dental Compliance Specialists.

Although I continue to help many "little guys" and love doing so, my time since 2011 has afforded me experience across the dental spectrum, from solo practitioners to large group practices, and everything in between.

As soon as I transferred from law enforcement to helping practices I realized the problems in the dental world were mostly caused by good people who just didn't know what they didn't know. They weren't intentionally violating compliance issues. They were doing their best and making honest mistakes. Day after day, I helped clean up messes made by honest mistakes. It was a startling contrast compared to my years as a law enforcement officer. The more practices I helped, the more I realized that I had an amazing opportunity to become an ally to people who really needed my help.

It broke my heart to see so many practices get slammed with legal troubles and scramble to climb out from the rubble. I knew there had to be a better way than waiting for practices to mess up and coming in to help them clean up the mess. I knew investigating after the fact was *not* the best policy. I'm a big believer of "An ounce of prevention beats a pound of cure."

Convincing busy dentists to invest in prevention, however, was not an easy task. With so many pulls on their attention, they barely had enough time to plan their day. The default seemed to be that it was simply easier for most people to buy pain relief than to invest in prevention.

Over the years, though, I've been fortunate to help enough dentists that word spread that prevention doesn't have to be complicated and can even make your day much simpler and easier. My clients became my billboards. My work became my marketing. Word spread that simple solutions exist for even many of the most complex compliance issues. And since that time, I've been able to help countless dental practices get more peace of mind, productivity, and profits.

I've seen dozens of practices get stuck underneath complicated solutions and pull their hair out trying to work through it. Sometimes the simplest solutions have the biggest impact.

But as the years went by, I realized that the same principles I applied to solo practitioners could apply to group practices as well. If you own a dental practice that's facing a legal battle, or you just want to stay ahead of it all, you're not alone. That's why I do what I do.

If you're wondering how, the first thing you ought to focus on is building systems. Like Glenn talked about in this book, make sure you and your team design systems and follow them, each and every day. Identify what parts don't work and revise them. This is one of the simplest yet most powerful ways to stay in compliance. The whole point of compliance isn't always about avoiding trouble—it's about not letting the possibility distract you and slow down your business.

Once you get your systems in place, it allows you to focus on things that actually matter. When you can't, you make mistakes. When you make mistakes, you get into trouble. One example that hurts me the most is about a dentist who mistakenly let an unlicensed tech perform an X-ray on a patient. The dental practice was put under investigation. and that dentist agreed to pay $9 million in damages.

That sounds like "pie in the sky," but it could happen to anyone. This happened because the practice was too distracted and stressed about the million other things to worry about, and something crucial slipped through the cracks. If you think you're stressed now, trust me, you don't want to know how you'll feel when you're under investigation.

The good news is if you apply just a fraction of what you learned in this book, you'll be far ahead of many practices out there. You'll develop the mindset of an owner. You'll build a team that cares and is careful. And you'll build systems that set you up for success over time.

As with clinical care, prevention is superior to treatment, but at Dental Compliance Specialists, we help with both. For many practices, the time you buy the most smoke detectors is right after your house burns down. For those practices, it's about being readily available when something goes wrong. We understand that's where some practices are starting.

For others, it's about systematically evaluating their business and identifying whether the organization is still on target to stay in compliance. Even if something does happen, partnering with a compliance officer will put your practice in a more favorable light in the investigation. If you're investing the time and effort to do things right, the government recognizes that you're doing your due diligence and will respond more leniently.

So, whether your record is spotless or you're trying to recover from an incident, a partner makes the difference between insecurity and confidence.

When you work with us, you remove the guesswork around compliance. You stop getting stressed and distracted by the possibility of trouble and, instead, focus on what moves the needle forward in your business. To us, eliminating that stress and distraction is what drives a positive ROI.

Above all, I don't want to see you wait until you're in trouble to establish a connection with a trusted authority in compliance. Compliance is just as important as performing cleanings and X-rays. When you know your compliance is secured, you feel peace of mind. Running a dental practice is already complex and dynamic, so don't make it more complicated. Be proactive and stay ahead of the game.

If you want to learn more about how we do what we do, visit dentalcompliance.com/pages/aboutus.

DUANE TINKER,
CEO of Dental Compliance Specialists

Appendix of Resources

Below are some dental resources from some of our Nifty Thrifty Dentists sponsors who helped make this book possible. Many members of my Nifty Thrifty Dentists community have benefitted from working with each of these people and companies and I highly recommend them.

Mango Voice (Get.MangoVoice.com/NiftyThrifty)
Mango Voice is a VoIP phone service created with security and efficiencies that dental practices need.

Crazy Dental Prices (CrazyDentalPrices.com/NiftyThrifty)
Thousands of satisfied members rely on Crazy Dental Prices for their dental supply needs due to the convenience of shopping online, coupled with exceptional customer service and lightning-fast shipping.

Duane Tinker (DentalCompliance.com)
Dental compliance solutions for dental offices and DSOs. Reach out to Duane and mention this book.

Jeff Guidie/4G Dental Lab (4GDentalLab.com)
4G Dental labs bring you high-quality lab work at a competitive price. Reach out and make sure you tell them you want the Nifty Thrifty pricing.

Wade Myers/GotaDental LLC (GotaDentalLLC.com)
Supplying doctors across the US with quality dental equipment solutions. Make sure you mention Nifty Thrifty Dentists.

Sean Ryan/Medidenta (NiftyMedidenta.com)
Medidenta continues to be at the forefront of dental technology with a product catalog that includes high-speed and low-speed handpieces, the CR Rated Prophy Magic award winning prophy angles, whitening products, and more.

Harsh Patel/HMP Consultants (HMPConsultants.com)
HMP Consultants provides various financial and business services to practices like yours, including accounting, bookkeeping, payroll, cash flow, part-time CFO services, tax consulting, cash flow management, and more.

About the Author

Dr. Glenn Vo is a thought leader in dentistry, a frequent speaker at national events, an investor in several businesses, and a full-time dentist in Texas.

He founded Nifty Thrifty Dentists to help dental professionals save money by negotiating discounts with the dental industry. The social network now has more than fifty-five thousand members while Glenn's podcast has been downloaded more than one million times.

From an early age while growing up in Pasadena, Texas, Glenn was a natural at building authentic relationships. He had plenty of flair as a waiter for TGI Friday's and also used his sales skills to melt diners' hearts into ordering extra cheese fondue at The Melting Pot. Dentistry, however, is his true profession. After attending the

Baylor College of Dentistry for his dental training, he later cofounded Denton Smiles Dentistry in Denton, Texas, with his wife, Susan Tran, in 2009.

Glenn realized while growing Denton Smiles that fellow private practitioners were missing out on deals from corporate dentistry, and he has since leveled the playing field through Nifty Thrifty Dentists. This experience also taught him the power of online promotion, which Glenn used to attract interest in his *USA Today* best-selling book *2612 Cherryhill Lane*. It also led to his second book, *Wall Street Journal* and *USA Today* best seller *Industry Influencer*, which guides readers through the steps of growing their brand through meaningful engagement and connection online.

Glenn is an active member of the Christian community. He has been inspired to funnel his passions for connection, writing, and making an impact into diverse projects, including becoming a partner in Morgan James Publishing and other media and publishing ventures.

When he's not writing books or helping patients, followers, and readers smile, Glenn's smiling along with his wife and their two children at their home in the Dallas–Fort Worth area.

A free ebook edition is available with the purchase of this book.

To claim your free ebook edition:

1. Visit MorganJamesBOGO.com
2. Sign your name CLEARLY in the space
3. Complete the form and submit a photo of the entire copyright page
4. You or your friend can download the ebook to your preferred device

Print & Digital Together Forever.

Snap a photo

Free ebook

Read anywhere